Ess Japan

by
DAVID SCOTT

David Scott is a food and travel writer and karate
instructor who specialises in Japan and the Far East.
He has written over 20 books and is a regular
contributor to a variety of newspapers and magazines.

AA

Produced by AA Publishing

Written by David Scott
Peace and Quiet section
by Paul Sterry
Original photography
by Douglas Corrance

Revised second edition January
1995
First published January 1992

Edited, designed and produced by
AA Publishing.
© The Automobile Association 1995.
Maps © The Automobile Association
1995.

Distributed in the United Kingdom
by AA Publishing, Norfolk House,
Priestley Road, Basingstoke,
Hampshire, RG24 9NY.

the information provided by the
same. Assessments of attractions,
hotels, restaurants and so forth are
based upon the author's own
experience and, therefore,
descriptions given in this guide
necessarily contain an element of
subjective opinion which may not
reflect the publisher's opinion or
dictate a reader's own experience
on another occasion.
**We have tried to ensure accuracy
in this guide, but things do
change and we would be grateful
if readers would advise us of any
inaccuracies they may encounter.**

Published by AA Publishing, a
trading name of Automobile
Association Developments Limited,
whose registered office is Norfolk
House, Priestley Road, Basingstoke,
Hampshire,
RG24 9NY.
Registered number 1878835.

Colour separation: Mullis Morgan
Ltd. London

Printed by: Printers Trento, S.R.L.,
Italy

*Front cover picture: child with
parasol*

Country Distinguishing
Signs

On some maps, international
distinguishing signs have
been used to indicate the
location of those countries
which surround Japan. Thus:

(CN) = China
(KP) = North Korea
(SU) = Russian Federation
(ROK) = South Korea
(RC) = Taiwan

This book employs a simple rating system to help choose which places to visit:

 'top ten'

◆◆◆ do not miss

◆◆ see if you can

◆ worth seeing if you have time

INTRODUCTION

Japan is a complex and fascinating country where an intriguing mixture of the old and new co-exist side by side. It is still a strange and sometimes confusing place for a foreigner to visit since the ways of the Japanese are unique to them, but almost all visitors leave Japan feeling enchanted and already planning for their return trip. It is a most interesting and exotic place to visit either on holiday or on business.

Japan is unusual in being, at the same time, a modern Western-style capitalist state with a

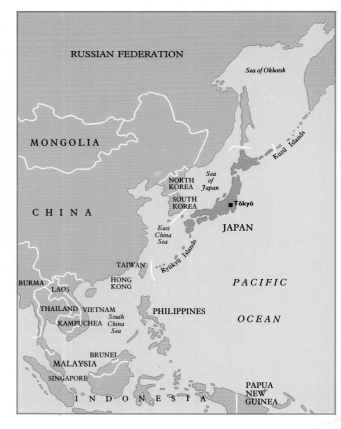

*The dazzling face of
modern Tōkyō*

successful economy, fast and efficient services
and an excellent communications network; and a
country which is free from petty crime,
dishonesty, drugs and for the most part litter.
Tourists can go anywhere at any time of the day
or night, even in busy city centres, and be sure
that they will be safe and the area will be clean.
This safety and hygiene allows the visitor a sense
of security that gives him or her the freedom to
really enjoy the constant surprises and the
uniqueness and beauty that Japan offers. You can
move easily between busy, prosperous cities
with all the culture and amenities you could want,
ranging from contemporary art galleries to
traditional Kabuki theatres, and hamburger
parlours to sushi bars; and remote country areas
with mountain views, ancient castles and
Buddhist temples where you will be welcomed
and where, for a small payment, you can spend
the night.

Japan is an expensive country but standards are
so high that even if you stay in the most modest
hotels, regularly eat in restaurants used by the
Japanese on a day-to-day basis and only travel
on the public transport network, you will still get
excellent service and have the opportunity to
thoroughly enjoy your visit on a budget and to
see as much of the country as you will wish to or
have the time for.

INTRODUCTION

The Japanese have embraced 20th-century technology and ideas, but they are still a people governed by traditional social values and etiquette. They are polite to one another and in the main treat one another with respect and graciousness. As a visitor you will be afforded the same civility and often an extra kindness, although in out of the way and country areas this will be mixed with curiosity and shyness.

Japan is made up of four main islands: Honshu in the centre, the most populous and developed; sub-tropical Kyūshū in the south; Shikoku, the smallest and least developed in the west; and Hokkaidō, where they have long cold winters, in the north. There are also many smaller islands, some located almost as far north as the coast of Russia and others, in the South China Sea, which lie as far south as Taiwan.

Most of the people live in huge, densely populated cities, many of which have developed along the edges of the flat, rice-growing plains and around the coastal bays of Honshū. In the main, Japanese cities have been poorly planned and they are often a mess of uncontrolled development. Nevertheless many do have a real fascination of their own and an energy and vibrancy that compensates for their lack of aesthetic appeal. There are also valuable exceptions, such as Kyōto and the modern high-technology city of Fukuoka in Kyūshū. Furthermore, the city authorities of places like Tōkyō and Osaka seem to have learned from past mistakes and their town planning policies are now directed as much towards environmental- and people-friendly issues as those of a purely financial nature.

Cities, however, occupy a relatively small part of Japan's land surface, the rest is steeply mountainous with only isolated pockets of flat, inhabited land. Northern and central Honshū, Hokkaidō and central Shikoku and Kyūshū offer plenty of scope for visiting remote and scenic wilderness areas.

All medium to large Japanese cities and many smaller ones have a tourist information office (often in or near the railway station) where even if the staff do not speak English they will have information in English on accommodation, places to visit and an English-language city map.

BACKGROUND

Old Japan

Until the end of World War II, mainland Japan had never been invaded successfully by a foreign power, and Japanese culture developed in an atmosphere of isolation. Japanese history has thus had a profound influence on the contemporary customs, beliefs, religious practices and manners of the Japanese people, and to understand them some knowledge of their history is essential.

From the 12th until the 16th century, Japan was subject to almost continuous civil war. Battles were fought between opposing clans seeking overall power or by emperors trying to gain a political control that matched their spiritual rule of the land. The situation improved in the late 16th century when General Oda Nobunaga defeated the most powerful clan leader in the country, General Imagawa, to become ruler of virtually all Japan. Nobunaga was both a ruthless soldier and a devotee of the arts. Under his guidance there was a renaissance of interest in poetry, theatre, dancing and fashion, which all flourished in the relative peace of his reign. He also encouraged trade with the outside world, and European arts and Christianity became

Itsukushima, an early Shinto shrine

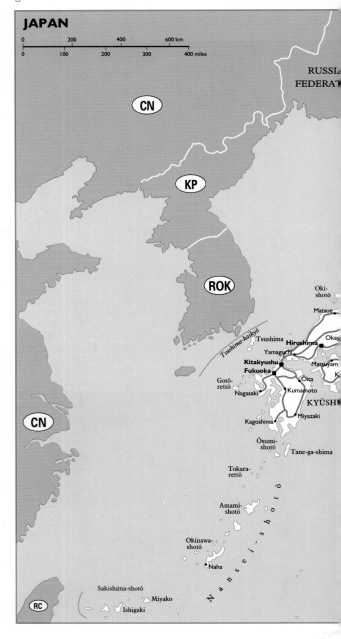

JAPAN

RUSSIAN
FEDERATION

CN

KP

ROK

CN

RC

Oki-shotō
Matsue
Tsushima-kaikyō
Tsushima
Hiroshima
Yamaguchi
Oka
Kitakyushu
Fukuoka
Matsuyam
Gotō-rettō
Ōita
K
Nagasaki
Kumamoto
KYŪSHŪ
Kagoshima
Miyazaki
Ōsumi-shotō
Tane-ga-shima
Tokara-rettō
Amami-shotō
Nansei-shotō
Okinawa-shotō
Naha
Sakishima-shotō
Miyako
Ishigaki

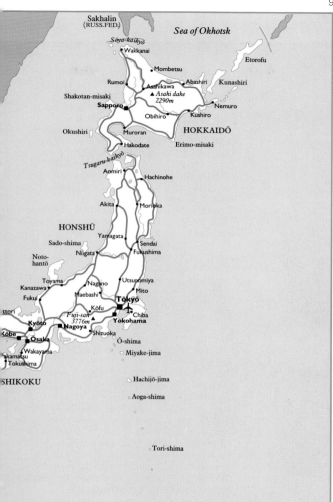

Sakhalin
(RUSS. FED.)

Sea of Okhotsk

Sōya-kaikyō

Wakkanai

Etorofu

Mombetsu

Rumoi · Abashiri · Kunashiri

Asahikawa

Shakotan-misaki ▲ *Asahi dake 2290m*

Sapporo Nemuro

Okushiri Obihiro Kushiro

HOKKAIDŌ

Muroran

Hakodate Erimo-misaki

Tsugaru-kaikyō

Aomori Hachinohe

Akita Morioka

HONSHŪ

Yamagata

Sado-shima Sendai

Noto-hantō Niigata Fukushima

Toyama Nagano Utsunomiya

Kanazawa Maebashi Mito

Fukui Kōfu **Tōkyō**

ttori Nagano

Kyōto *Fuji-san 3776m* Chiba

Kōbe **Nagoya** **Yokohama**

Ōsaka Shizuoka

akamatsu Wakayama Ō-shima

Tokushima Miyake-jima

SHIKOKU

Hachijō-jima

Aoga-shima

Tori-shima

Ogasawara-guntō

Kazan-rettō

fashionable. He was less generous at home and declared war on a number of Buddhist sects which he believed were divisive and warmongering influences. He ordered the complete destruction of a complex of monasteries on Mount Hiei, a religious centre near Kyōto, and the death of all the monks, mainly by burning. Nobunaga in his turn was murdered by one of his own generals. The killing took place in a temple where Nobunaga was performing in a Noh play and was in retaliation for an assumed insult.

Toyotomi Hideyoshi succeeded to power in 1582. He had a different outlook from Nobunaga and thought that foreign influences were weakening the spirit of the Japanese nation. He slowly introduced laws aimed at reducing the influx of foreign goods and people and at the same time reinforced traditional feudal patterns of society.

Hideyoshi gradually subdued all the remaining outposts of independent clan leaders and by 1590 was the ruler of a united Japan. Through the changes he instituted in the government of the nation, Japan gradually became more insular and rigidly feudal.

Hideyoshi died in 1598 and was succeeded by Tokugawa Ieyasu, who moved his headquarters from Kyōto to Edo (now Tōkyō). From here the Tokugawa family dominated Japanese life for the next 250 years. One after another the Tokugawa shoguns maintained a hostility to all foreign religions and secular influences, and carried out a policy of national seclusion. Japanese were prohibited from travelling outside the country and foreigners were not allowed in. The laws that were enacted during the Tokugawan era (1603–1868) help to explain many contemporary Japanese attitudes.

The intention of the Tokugawa shoguns was to control every aspect of Japanese life in every corner of the land. The place a person lived, what he ate, the type of clothes he wore, the style of language he used, even the posture he adopted and the way he slept were dictated by the state. A succession of Tokugawa shoguns tightened up the already rigid Japanese class system and used the division of the people into classes as a method for maintaining and

*Shogun Minamoto
Jorimoto*

perpetuating their own power. The arts
continued to flourish, however, and life was
relatively peaceful and secure for common folk
as long as the rules were obeyed and there was
enough to eat.

The emperor had no power by this time and he
and his court were restricted to Kyōto. The
Tokugawa shogun maintained the position of
emperor in order that he could confer the title on
whoever the family selected, and the emperor's
duties were confined to the purely ceremonial.
The rest of society was split into four groups. In
descending order of status they were samurai,
farmers, craftsmen and merchants. Women
belonged to the same class as their fathers or
husbands. Membership of a particular class was
hereditary. The samurai did not work as such
and they considered the pursuit of money

dishonourable. They were supported by taxes from the farming class, who suffered considerable hardship maintaining the top-heavy warrior class. The samurai enjoyed many privileges and during the Tokugawa years had little to do since there were few battles to fight. They were, however, expected to set a good example to the rest of society and to lead sober and honest lives. In this time of peace the samurai brought the arts of fighting to a high point of skill, ceremonial and ritual, although expertise in real battle fighting and war tactics diminished.

Merchants were at the bottom of the social ladder since they did not produce anything and worse than that, they were motivated by profit and dealt with money. In spite of their lowly position in the social order, the merchant class later became the main beneficiaries of the Tokugawa era and as a group they were largely responsible for later changes in cultural and social attitudes.

The Tokugawa system of government began to break down by the late 18th century. The samurai had been emasculated by lack of opportunity to do battle. They had become as interested in the arts of the tea ceremony and calligraphy as in that of sword fighting, and had lost their authoritarian grip on the country. Both they and the peasants had grown very poor and the newly prosperous merchant class had emerged as a force for change. Because of their influence Western explorers and traders had been allowed to enter Japan again. In 1867 the young Emperor Meiji ended the long cloistered existence of the Imperial family by putting himself forward as the country's leader. He became the focal point for a Japanese nation that had lost its cohesion. After fighting off Tokugawa loyalists he attained full power in 1868 and began his revolutionary reign, the Meiji Restoration.

Emperor Meiji for the first time formally instigated Shinto as the official religion. Since the Shinto belief is that the emperor is of divine lineage and a living god, this new ruling gave him total power over the nation. He used it primarily to abolish the old class system and to institute new laws and reforms that were intended to give more human rights to all Japanese. From this beginning Emperor Meiji led Japan over the next 40 years from being an isolated, agriculturally based, feudal society to a powerful nation with a modern navy and army, good railways, a parliament and an industrial base. The changes he wrought were not without their excesses, however, since the Japanese seem to be unable to make gradual changes. Things Japanese were despised for a period and many historical buildings and relics destroyed. At the same time the North American and European cultures were admired. During this period there was even a cult for marrying Western women in order to improve the nation's bloodstock. During the Meiji era Japan won the Sino-Japanese war in 1895–98 and defeated the Russians in the Japanese-Russian war of 1904–5.

Modern Japan

By the beginning of the 1930s Japan's industrial economy needed overseas markets and new sources of raw materials. At the same time there was an upsurge of nationalism and a growing sense that Japan was the natural leader of mainland Asia and the Pacific basin. Both factors led Japan to invade Manchuria in 1931, followed by a full-scale invasion of China in 1937. They withdrew from the League of Nations and at home totalitarian politics and militarism grew in popularity. The movement was unlike the fascism of Italy and Germany since the emperor remained the secular and spiritual head of the state around whom a consensus form of government was centred. The Japanese were, however, to join forces with Hitler, and on 7 December 1941, with the bombing of Pearl Harbor, they entered World War II.

Japan's subsequent military defeat was followed by the Allied occupation. A ruined economy and the devastation of most of its major cities forced Japan into another period of rapid change. The Japanese were economically and spiritually broken by their first military defeat in history and by the horrific way in which the war was finally ended with the atomic destruction of two major cities, Hiroshima and Nagasaki. A new start was required and a re-examination of national values was undertaken at every level.

BACKGROUND

Shinto is part of everyday life

After the war the Japanese parliamentary system was revised to become a constitutional democracy. The prime minister is elected from the ruling party in the National Diet. The constitution forbids the use or development of nuclear arms and the formation of an army for reasons other than defence. It expressly denies the emperor any political power. He is defined as the symbol of the state and derives his position only from the will of the people. Civil liberties are wide-ranging and written into the constitution. The voting age is 20. Japan's desire for expansion has been concentrated on industry and international trade, and her success in these areas is matched by an increase in the standard of living, high employment and improving social welfare at home.

Because of their history the Japanese people have developed certain unique qualities that perhaps explain their economic success in the last 50 years. They manage to combine a sense of mutual responsibility, honesty and loyalty together with competitiveness. These attributes are merged with an unquestioning acceptance of long working hours and an enthusiastic commitment to job and employer. On top of this, they have developed a keen understanding of the needs of specific home and overseas markets and the ability to fulfil them. The Japanese government have simultaneously protected their own market from foreign competitors by imposing rigorous import quotas and duties.

The Japanese have moved a long way since America's Commodore Perry and his black ships opened Japan to the outside world. In those days the Western nation had enormous influence on Japan, now it is very much a two-way process. There are even clear indications that in the future Japan will become the most dominant force, more influential than the United States and Europe in shaping Western economies and attitudes.

Religion

Shinto is a religion unique to Japan, and its beliefs have influenced Japanese history and the Japanese character. Known by the Japanese as *Kami-No-Machi*, the 'Way of the Gods', Shinto has its origins in the myths of the tribal people of ancient Japan. They believed that in all the world only their islands were populated and that they themselves were the children of the gods. Followers of Shinto worship the spirit of the god Kami, whose nature is manifested in all the things around them such as rivers, mountains, trees, rocks and animals. Each deity has a place in a hierarchy of power which culminates in the sun goddess Amaterasu. Amaterasu is worshipped at the imperial shrines of Ise on the Shima Peninsula on Honshū where the spirits of all past emperors are enshrined. Lesser deities are the local *kami* who look after just one village or one family's fields.

Shinto shrines are to be found throughout Japan in cities and countryside alike. *Jinja*, as they are called in Japanese, are constructed from unpainted wood and often have thatched roofs. In the countryside small, rudimentary *jinja* are found marking a particular field or a local beauty spot. The Japanese make offerings at a *jinja* either to their ancestors or to the guardian spirits of the particular shrine. This is a commonplace activity and city shrines are busy places with people going in and out all day. There is a water trough by the inner shrine, and before making an offering the worshipper pours water over his hands and rinses his mouth. After this symbolic purification he attracts the gods by clapping his hands three times and pulling on a rope attached to a wooden clapper on the ceiling of the shrine. A silent prayer is then given and an offering of fruit, money, incense or *nusa* (small strips of white paper symbolizing purity, sold at the shrine entrance) is made. You may enjoy following the ritual yourself.

The entrance to a *jinja* is easily identified by a gate with two uprights and two crossbars, known as a *torii* gate, guarded on either side by a carved stone lion-dog. The mouth of one dog is open and the other is closed. They symbolize the sounds 'Ah' of birth and 'Mm' of death. A visitor to the shrine passes between the dogs and is reminded that the line between life and death is a short one.

There are no fixed scriptures in Shinto. Its rituals and ceremonies are directed at receiving a blessing from the gods for a particular function or event. They are a daily part of Japanese life. Shinto priests, wearing long flowing robes and tall lacquered silk hats in a style unchanged for a thousand years, are called upon to officiate at all manner of occasions. Ceremonies are held to bless babies, marriages, children starting school, new construction sites, even new cars. The priest carries a pine branch (*sakaki*) which he waves over the subject of the ceremony as a sign of purification and blessing.

Confucianism, brought to Japan by Chinese merchants, had an important influence on Shinto beliefs. This is still evident in the traditions of contemporary Japanese society. Confucianism, was a code of ethics which emphasised loyalty to the family, with the father as patriarchal head, as one of its most important rules. The first-born son directly succeeded his father. Mothers were to be respected and loved. Ancestors were to be revered and their memories respected. Loyalty was one of the highest virtues.

These ideas, coupled with Shinto teachings that the emperor was a living *kami* and that the spirits of the dead lived on, produced the patriarchal, ancestor-worshipping culture of traditional Japan. The emperor as a living god was given allegiance by the nation. He was the symbolic and literal father of the one family of the Japanese

Japanese priest officiating at a burial

people. Such beliefs lived on until World War II, when the Japanese suicide squads sacrificed their lives for the emperor. This influence is still evident in the patriarchal attitude of Japanese companies towards their workforce, and the loyalty of their employees. Followers of Shinto do not see its beliefs or practices as an obstacle to following other religions. In some Japanese households you may see a Shinto offering to the ancestors, a Buddhist statue and a Christian crucifix all collected together in one room for worship.

Shinto, with its emphasis on the basic purity of all things, was fertile ground for the assimilation of Buddhist and especially Zen Buddhist beliefs. The two schools of thought have never merged, but the majority of Japanese subscribe to both. In fact many Buddhist temples either contain within their grounds, or are adjacent to, a Shinto shrine. The Japanese use rituals from one or the other to mark important events in their lives. For instance, marriage is usually a Shinto ceremony and burial a Buddhist one. In daily life the practice of followers of both Zen and Shinto is to be pure in heart and accepting of the changing nature of all things.

Men and Women
Not many years ago Japanese women were under a lot of family and social pressure to marry

by their early twenties. There was heated competition for men and the bridal schools did a good business in teaching young women how to cook, sew and to be feminine.

The situation nowadays is different and continuing to change. The financial freedom gained by many women through Japan's commercial success, the influence of Western ideas, urbanisation and the loss by men, to their corporation jobs, of their individual freedoms has created a new chapter in Japanese history. Nowadays, women are no longer in a rush to get married and some men, pushed off their pedestals, are beginning to feel unsure about their roles in life and their relationships with women. *Hanayome Gakko* (bridal schools) are now matched by *Hanamoko Gakko* (bridegroom schools) where courses are offered to help men better understand women.

The daily ritual of commuting to work

WHAT TO SEE

Introduction

Japan is a complex network of different islands, cities, mountains and lakes and the Japanese divide it geographically into many different areas, regions, prefectures, sub-prefectures and so on. For the tourist it is a confusing and complicated task to try and understand and remember the relationships between place names and regions and to locate a particular spot on the map. The situation is made more difficult by the tendency of different guide books to divide the country in a variety of ways. To simplify matters, *Essential Japan* has divided the country along the lines of the compass into six major areas, each sub-divided into their major cities and/or geographical features.

TŌKYŌ, KAMAKURA AND FUJI-SAN (MOUNT FUJI)

TŌKYŌ

Tōkyō is one of the world's largest cities and certainly one of the most dynamic, but on first impressions it seems to be without any particular distinguishing features. More than superficial investigation, however, reveals it to be a complex metropolis formed by a series of connected towns or districts each with its own individual neighbourhoods, character and energy. By getting to know them and their geographical relationship to each other the city becomes easier to understand.

The area of Tōkyō of most interest to the tourist is that bounded by the JR Yamanote loop line. Within this circle most of the places you will wish to visit are easily reached by subway taxi or on foot. (See **Subways**, page 123 and **Taxis**, page 124). The best times to visit Tōkyō are late March to early May and in the autumn. Avoid mid-June to the end of August when it is very humid.

Main Districts

The great earthquake of 1923 and, later, the Allied bombing of World War II destroyed most of Tōkyō's traditional buildings, but a flavour of old Japan and its popular culture can be experienced in the **Ueno** and **Asakusa** districts in the northeast of the city. Ueno Park is the cultural heart of Tōkyō and most of the nation's major art galleries and museums are found in its grounds, as well as the zoo that houses Japan's prized giant pandas. Asakusa is a temple town and home of the famous Kannon Temple, a popular visiting place during holidays and festivals. North of Ueno is **Yanaka** where the flimsy wooden houses and temples have somehow escaped the bulldozer. The old streets are a favourite haunt of photographers and artists.

In the centre of Tōkyō is the monumental 19th-century **Imperial Palace**, the seat of the Emperor and the spiritual focus of all Japan. There are fascinating walks in the environs of the palace, but access to the actual grounds is restricted to New Year's Day and the Emperor's

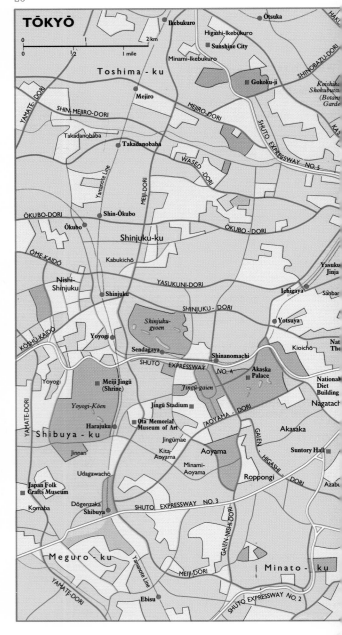

TŌKYŌ

Ikebukuro

Ōtsuka

Higashi-Ikebukuro

Sunshine City

Minami-Ikebukuro

Toshima-ku

Gokoku-ji

Mejiro

MEJIRO-DORI

Koishika
Shokubutsi
(Botani
Garde

SHIN-MEJIRO-DORI

YAMATE-DORI

Takadanobaba

Takadanobaba

WASEDA-DORI

SHUTO EXPRESSWAY NO.5

KAS

Yamanote Line

MEIJI-DORI

ŌKUBO-DORI

Shin-Ōkubo

ŌKUBO - DORI

Ōkubo

Shinjuku-ku

ŌME-KAIDŌ

Kabukichō

Yasuku
Jinja

Nishi-
Shinjuku

YASUKUNI-DORI

Ichigaya

Sanbar

Shinjuku

SHINJUKU - DORI

KŌSHŪ-KAIDŌ

Yotsuya

Yoyogi

Shinjuku-
gyoen

Sendagaya

Kioichō

Nat
The

SHUTO EXPRESSWAY

Shinanomachi

NO.4

Akasaka
Palace

National
Diet
Building

YAMATE-DORI

Yoyogi

Meiji Jingū
(Shrine)

Jingū-gaien

Nagatach

Yoyogi-Kōen

Jingū Stadium

AOYAMA - DORI

Harajuku

Ota Memorial
Museum of Art

Shibuya - ku

Jinnan

Jingūmae

Kita-
Aoyama

Aoyama

Akasaka

GAIEN HIGASHI

Suntory Hall

Japan Folk
Crafts Museum

Udagawachō

Minami-
Aoyama

Roppongi

DORI

Azab

Komaba

Dōgenzaka

Shibuya

SHUTO EXPRESSWAY NO. 3

GAIEN-NISHI-DORI

Meguro - ku

Yamanote Line

MEIJI-DORI

Minato - ku

YAMATE-DORI

Ebisu

SHUTO EXPRESSWAY NO. 2

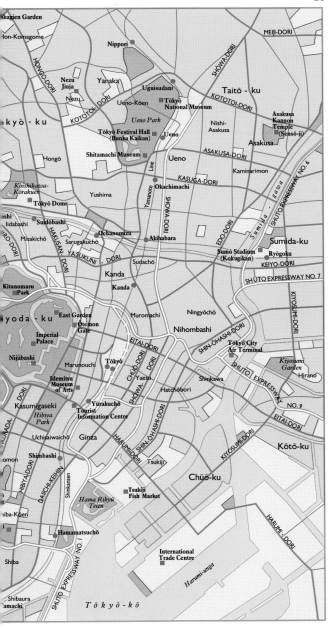

birthday. Around the perimeter of the palace are the rather soulless government districts of **Kasumigaseki** and **Nagatachō** where the **National Diet Building** (parliament) and government ministry buildings are found. Further east is the **Ginza**, an area of huge department stores (*depāto*) (including Seibu, said to be the 'state of the art' *depāto*), boutiques and expense account restaurants. The streets of the Ginza are normally full of shoppers or evening socialisers. To the southwest of the palace is **Akasaka** district and further on, on the western edge of the area bounded by the Yamanote Line, are **Shinjuku** and **Harajuku**. **Roppongi** on the Hibaya Line is perhaps the city's most cosmopolitan area and the centre of its nightlife. More expensive and sophisticated, Akasaka is a focus for the business community and is an area of good (expensive) hotels, restaurants and nightclubs. The elegant and chic **Aoyama** district next to Akasaka is home to the shops of Tōkyō's fashion superstars such as Issey Miyake and Yohji Yamamoto. Shinjuku started life as a characterless satellite city within a city and gained a reputation for rowdyness and sleazy nightlife. It has in the main outgrown this image and outside the incredibly complex and seemingly chaotic Shinjuku Subway Sation are to be found good department stores, gift shops and boutiques and perfectly respectable restaurants and bars. However, the **Kabukichō** area within Shinjuku district is still the place to go for the seedy massage parlours and

cheap dives. Harajuku is a district of contrasts. It is both the centre of a hysterical teen fashion scene and the site of the historically important and beautiful Meiji Shrine.

Tips on Tōkyō

● Before going to Japan contact the nearest Japanese National Tourist Organization office in your country (see page 124) and ask them for their tourist maps of Japan and Tōkyō.

● If you do not book accommodation in Tōkyō in advance, ensure you arrive in the city in time to visit a Tourist Information Centre (TIC) office. There are two at Narita Airport and one in the city centre (see page 124). They will help you find a suitable place.

● As soon as you arrive in Tōkyō obtain, either from a TIC office or from any large railway station, an English-language subway map.

● Before deciding what to do in the city, get a free copy of Tōkyō *Tour Companion*, a weekly English-language newspaper for tourists, and buy a copy of the monthly Tōkyō *Journal*, an up-to-date informative publication in English. Both these publications contain details of current events. Both are available at the TIC offices and large hotels.

● For taped information (in English) on current events phone 3503–2911.

● The Tōkyō English Life Line is on 3264–4347. They will help with personal problems.

● For practical advice and information on hotels, restaurants etc, ring the city centre TIC on 3502-1461.

Crowds at Asakusa Kannon Temple

WHAT TO SEE

◆◆◆
ASAKUSA KANNON TEMPLE (SENSO-JI) ✓

2–3–1, Asakusa, Taito-ku
Tōkyō's oldest temple (although the present buildings are replicas of those destroyed in World War II). A place held in great affection by Tokyoites, the temple grounds are usually crowded, especially on festival days. According to legend it was founded in 628 by two fishermen who had netted a statue of Kannon (a Buddhist saint of compassion) in a nearby river. Inside the entrance to the temple grounds is an arcaded street lined with shops selling souvenirs, food and traditional gifts.
Open: 24 hours
Subway station: Asakusa
General location: Asakusa, northern Tōkyō

◆◆
HARAJUKU DISTRICT
Every Sunday, along the broad avenue forming the south perimeter of Yoyogi-kōen (Park) near JR Harajuku Station dozens of Japanese rock bands set up their amplifiers and instruments and give free open-air concerts. They compete with one another for air space and the noise is cacophonous. They are accompanied by James Dean lookalike rock-and-roll fans with greased black hair wearing thick, crêpe-soled shoes and drain-pipe jeans, and very young girls with bouffant hairstyles, dayglo dancing pumps and short, flared skirts. They dance together in sequence and the rebellion is just show. Food stalls, roller skate dancers, traditional drummers and all sorts of fringe people add to the fun.

Takeshita-dori nearby is a cramped alleyway where cheap boutiques and stall-holders sell sunglasses, posters, badges and cut-rate fashion clothes. A young teenager's dream!
Subway station: Omotesando or JR Harajuku
General location: western Tōkyō

◆◆
IDEMITSU MUSEUM OF ARTS
Kokusai Building, 9th Floor, 3–1–1, Marunouchi, Chiyoda-ku
An excellent collection of Zen calligraphy and ink paintings, especially by Zen monk Sengai, and Japanese and Chinese

Fresh air in the city: Imperial Palace

ceramics and lacquerware. The galleries are very pleasant, well lit and some of their large windows overlook the Imperial Palace. There is a Japanese-style tea room. A fascinating but relaxed place for a leisurely visit.
Open: Tuesday to Sunday 10.00–17.00 hrs
Closed: Monday (or Tuesday if Monday is a national holiday) and 1–10 January
Subway station: Hibiya
General location: Imperial Palace, eastern Tōkyō

IMPERIAL PALACE
Chiyoda, Chiyoda-ku

The Imperial Palace is home to the Emperor. The residence and extensive grounds are situated right in the heart of Tōkyō. They are by far the most valuable pieces of real estate in the world. The actual palace is closed to the public, but the **East Garden** and adjacent **Kitanomaru Park** are open. Both are popular with Japanese and foreign tourists, and with Tokyoites who want some air and a stroll in the sunlight in the middle of a busy day in the concrete city.

Open: East Garden, Tuesday to Thursday, Saturday and Sunday 09.00–16.00 hrs (last entry 15.00 hrs)
Closed: Monday and Friday, and 25 December to 3 January; also if there is an Imperial ceremony
Subway station: Otemachi
General location: central Tōkyō.

JAPAN FOLK CRAFTS MUSEUM
4–3–33, Komaba, Meguro-ku

The late Yanagi Soetsu, the founder of the Japanese folk art movement, opened this museum to house his great collection of craft objects. The exhibits are displayed in a replica of a traditional Japanese farmhouse.

Open: Tuesday to Sunday 10.00–17.00 hrs
Closed: Monday (or Tuesday if Monday is a national holiday), 22 December to 3 January and all February
Subway station: Komaba-Todaimae, Keio-Inokashira Line
General location: Shibuya, southwestern Tōkyō.

MEIJI JINGŌ (SHRINE)
1–1, Yoyogi, Kamizono-cho, Shibuya-ku

Emperor Meiji (1853–1912) reigned during the period of Japan's transformation from an isolated nation unchanged for many hundreds of years into a modern world power. He and his wife Empress Shoken are buried near Kyōto, but this shrine was completed in his memory in 1920. It was destroyed in an air raid in 1945 but rebuilt in 1958. The grounds are thickly wooded, and also contain a famous **Iris Garden** once frequented by the Emperor and his consort. It is a beautiful and cool retreat, even during Tōkyō's hot, humid summer months. The approach to the shrine is spanned by a huge *torri* gate of cypress wood. Inside, a hall and long cloister constructed of unadorned wood provide an unobtrusive but elegant shelter from the elements. The shrine is very popular during the New Year festival, and on New Year's Eve trains run to the nearest JR station throughout the night.

Open: Shrine and Inner Garden, every day sunrise to sunset, except the third Friday of each month. Iris Garden, 1 March to 3 November 09.00–16.30 hrs, otherwise 09.00–16.00 hrs
Subway station: Meiji-Jingumae
JR Station: Harajuku and Yoyogi
General location: Shibuya, southwestern Tōkyō.

OTA MEMORIAL MUSEUM OF ART
1–10–10, Jingumae, Shibuya-ku

Seizo Ota, former chairman of Tōkyō Mutual Life, in the tradition

of successful Japanese entrepreneurs, bequeathed this superb collection of woodblock prints (*ukiyo-e*) to this private museum.
Open: Tuesday to Sunday 10.30–17.30 hrs
Closed: Monday (or Tuesday if Monday is a national holiday) and every month from 25th to the end of the month, and 1 December to 3 January
Subway station: Meiji-Jingumae
General location: Harajuku, southwestern Tōkyō

RIKUGIEN GARDEN
6–16–3, Honkomagome, Bunkyō-ku
Begun in 1695 by Lord Yanagisawa who had a taste for literature, the name of the garden means 'six types of poem garden'. Each of the particularly scenic spots in it has a literary reference. This is one of Tōkyō's most beautiful gardens and its best surviving example of an Edo-style strolling garden. In true Japanese style, Rikugien is artificial and contrived but nevertheless 'feels' natural.
Open: Tuesday to Sunday 09.00–16.15 hrs
Closed: Monday and 29 December to 3 January
Subway station: Sugamo or Komagome
JR Station: Komagome
General location: Ikebukuro, northern Tōkyō

ROPPONGI
Roppongi Station on Hibaya Line
Roppongi is grey and drab during the day, but by night it is transformed into Tōkyō's party town. It is worth a visit just to watch the people. Stand at Roppongi's crossing near the subway station and watch hordes of wildly dressed teenagers and singles on their way to bars, clubs or discos or just to parade up and down the neon-lit streets.
Open: seven nights a week!
General location: southern Tōkyō

SHITAMACHI MUSEUM
2–1, Ueno-Kōen, Taitō-ku
Shitamachi became the downtown or working-class area of Tōkyō between the earthquake of 1923 and World War II. After the war, with increasing prosperity, the characteristic nature of the area slowly started to disappear. In the late 1960s, in order to keep a record of their heritage, local pressure groups persuaded the district government to build this museum. There are accurate reconstructions of an ordinary merchant's house (look out for the bamboo basket hanging from the ceiling in which valuables were packed and carried in the event of a fire), an old schoolhouse, a tenement house with copper-smith's workshop, and a small sweet shop. There are many ordinary day-to-day objects on display and there is an emphasis on authenticity and visitor involvement. (See also **Yanaka** below).
Open: Tuesday to Sunday 09.30–16.30 hrs
Closed: Monday and 29 December to 3 January
Subway stations: Ueno and Yushima
General location: Ueno, northern Tōkyō.

◆◆◆
TŌKYŌ NATIONAL MUSEUM ✓

13–9, Ueno-Kōen, Taitō-ku
The museum consists of four main galleries and houses the finest collection of Japanese art in the world. The buildings are not exciting and the display conditions in the main hall are particularly poor, but the treasures on view make a visit worthwhile. The **Gallery of Horyuji Treasures**, one of the galleries, is open only on Thursdays (closed even then if it is heavily raining or very humid). It contains rare and priceless Buddhist artefacts and works of art from the Horyuji

Watching the world go by....

...Intriguing figures on display at theTōkyō National Museum

Temple in Nara, said to be the birthplace of Japanese Buddhism. The **Toyokan Gallery of Oriental Antiquities** specialises in archeological, historical and cultural objects from China, southeast-Asia and India.
Open: Tuesday to Sunday 09.00–16.30 hrs
Closed: Monday (or Tuesday if Monday is a national holiday) and 25 December to 3 January
JR station: Ueno
General location: Ueno Park, northern Tōkyō.

◆◆◆
TSUKIJI FISH MARKET ✓

5–2, Tsukiji, Chou-ku
Tsukiji is one of the most
fascinating places to visit in
Tōkyō, but it opens before dawn
and business is almost over by
09.30hrs, so many tourists miss
the opportunity of going. It is
definitely worth an early call and
a taxi ride from your hotel if the
subway is not convenient. In the
outer, smaller area of the market
are stalls and shops providing
everything for the catering trade
from bonito fish flakes to
personalised toothpicks. There
are also small cafés, bars and
coffee-shops serving the fish-
sellers, buyers and truckmen.
They are the places to go for
breakfast after a visit to the inner
market. The inner market is a
scene of mayhem and anarchy.
Streams of buyers and sellers
compete for space in numerous
alleyways crowded with men
pushing and pulling carts.
Open: Monday to Saturday
Closed: Sunday
Subway station: Tsukiji, Hibiya
Line
General location: Ginza,
southeastern Tōkyō

◆◆◆
YANAKA DISTRICT
Yanaka neighbourhood is north
of the **Shitamachi Museum** (see
page 26). It escaped most of the
destruction of the 1923
earthquake and World War II
bombing and preserves much of
the flavour of a Shitamachi
(working class) area. It has a
rustic atmosphere and a complex
network of streets of old houses,
shops and temples. It is worth
exploring on foot if you do not
mind getting lost. JR Nippori
Station on the Yamanote Line
provides a starting-off point.
General location: northeastern
Tōkyō

Serried ranks at the fish market

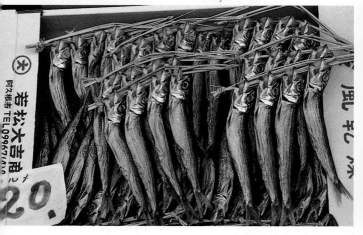

Accommodation

Tōkyō has a wide variety of accommodation available throughout the city, but those hotels near a central location are obviously the most convenient. The best locations and those areas with most major hotels are Akasaka, Ginza, Shinbashi and around Tōkyō Station. Book in advance for luxury-class hotels and for all hotels during major festivals and the month of February, when students arrive in Tōkyō to take their university entrance exams.

Of the first-class hotels the **New Otani**, 4-1, Kioicho, Chiyoda-ku (tel: (03) 3265-1111), is the largest, and it also retains one of Tōkyō's most beautiful gardens. The **Capitol Tokyu**, 2–10–3, Nagatacho, Chiyoda-ku (tel: (03) 3581-4511), which is in the heart of the government district, is surrounded by unusual quietness after office hours and it offers a welcome refuge after a noisy day in the city. For excellent views and quality post-war architecture the **Akasaka Prince**, 1-2, Kioicho, Chiyoda-ku (tel: (03) 3234-1111), is highly recommended.

To find a traditional Japanese *ryokan* (inn) in Tōkyō is nowadays quite rare, to find one that is not too expensive is almost impossible. The **Tokiwa Ryokan**, 7-27-9, Shinjuku, Shinjuku-ku (tel: (03) 3202-4321), close to Shinjuku Sanchome Station, offers Japanese (*ryokan*) and Western-style accommodation. The *ryokan* part is simple but with character. Good value and fine food if wished.

For information on all the types of accommodation available in Japan see **Accommodation**, pages 97–8. Note that whichever class of hotel you choose, standards of hygiene and service are normally good.

Entertainment

The comments made in **Culture, Entertainment and Nightlife**, pages 100–1, apply very much to Tōkyō. This section should also be referred to for details and listings on traditional performing arts. Tōkyō's nightlife is limitless, and many of the working population (known as 'salarimen' and 'office ladies') go straight from the office to a bar or club for a drink and a chat before either going home or continuing an evening carousing. The night starts early, at about 18.00 hrs, but also for most ends before midnight. At this hour night owls and young people about town head for **Roppongi** (see page 26), where the clubs and discos stay open to the early hours of the morning. For respectable entertainment the Ginza, Asakusa and Akasaka districts provide everything from neon-lit dazzle to the traditional singing, dancing and *samisen* (guitar) playing of kimono-clad geisha. For a more risqué night out Shinjuku and more especially its Kabukichō area, and the smaller Dogenzaka in Shibuya provide as many massage parlours, sleazy bars and strip joints as you would wish. Costs are high in these places and they are not aesthetically pleasing. But even here, as elsewhere, you do not need to worry unduly about your physical safety or the unlawful loss of your wallet. For cinema, theatre and other events the monthly *Tōkyō Journal*, available in your hotel, at the city or airport TIC offices or English-language bookshops, gives comprehensive listings and details of performances, as well as restaurant reviews and up-to-the-minute information on events of possible interest to English-speaking foreigners.

Restaurants

For the Japanese, and especially Tokyoites, eating out is an integral part of everyday life and many people eat more often in restaurants than they do at home. As a result there is an enormous variety of eating establishments in Tōkyō and something to suit every taste and pocket.

The traditions of Japanese food and the various classes and types of restaurant are detailed and discussed in **Food and Drink** (see pages 89–96). Some recommended restaurants are listed below, but the high density of establishments, coupled with the size of Tōkyō, means that eating out for most people is usually a matter of exploring the area in the vicinity of their accommodation. One special suggestion, however, is to visit the Tsukiji Fish Market (see page 28) one morning and stay on for an early lunch of sushi. The sushi bars near the market sell the freshest sushi you are ever likely to taste. The sushi-san prepares it with fish bought that morning. In the winter, eaten with hot sake, it makes the perfect lunch.

The restaurants listed in the first section are those places popular with and frequented by the Japanese and those in which you will only just manage without a Japanese friend or any knowledge of the language. Those in the second section are recommended by the Japanese National Tourist Organisation. They serve good food, mainly at reasonable prices, and the staff can cope with foreigners.

Botan (sukiyaki) 1–15, Kandasuda-chu, Chiyoda-ku (tel: (03) 3251-0577). In an attractive old building.

Chinya (sukiyaki and shabu-shabu) 1–3–4, Asakusa, Taito-ku (tel: (03) 3841-0010).

Daini's Table (Chinese nouvelle cuisine) San Trope Minami Aoyama, Basement, 6–3–14, Minami Aoyama, Minato-ku (tel: (03) 3407-0363).

Goemon (tofu) 1–1–26, Hon-komagome, Bunkyō-ku (tel: (03) 3811-2015). A Kyōto-style tofu restaurant.

Honke Ponta (tonkatsu pork) 3–23–2, Ueno, Taito-ku (tel: (03) 3831-2351). The oldest tonkatsu restaurant in Tōkyō.

Kamakura (yakitori) 4–10–11, Roppongi, Minato-ku (tel: (03) 3405-4377).

La Patata (Italian) 2–9–11, Jingūmae, Shibuya-ku (tel: (03) 3403-9664). An expensive restaurant with a pleasant atmosphere and good food.

Mamiana Soba (soba) 3–5–6, Azabudai, Minato-ku (tel: (03) 3583-0545). In an old house with attractive garden.

Tokyo Joe's (American) Akasaka Eight-One Building, 1st Basement, 2–13–5, Nagatacho, Chiyoda-ku (tel: (03) 3508-0325). Even some of the ingredients are flown in from Florida. Good service but very expensive.

Yabu Soba (soba) 2–10,

Awajicho, Kanda, Chiyoda-ku
(tel: (03) 3251-0287). Serves the
most celebrated soba in Tōkyō .
Very expensive.

Good Tourist Restaurants

Bell (Western) 1–29–9, Asakusa,
Taitō-ku (tel: (03) 3841-8303).
Cafeteria Cafe (coffee-shop)
2–1–1, Nishi-Shinjuku, Shinjuku-
ku (tel: (03) 3344-6969).
Doutor (coffee-shop) 4–8–10,
Ueno, Taitō-ku (tel: (03) 3831-
2586).
Funabenkei (general Japanese)
1–15–1, Shibuya, Shibuya-ku (tel:
(03) 3406-3033).
Genrokuzushi (sushi) 5–8–5,
Jingumae, Shibuya-ku (tel: (03)
3498-3968).
Genrokuzushi (sushi) 1–30–4,
Asakusa, Taitō-ku (tel: (03) 3845-
6157).
Ichimatsu (general Japanese)
1–15–1, Kiminarimon, Taitō-ku
(tel: (03) 3844-6262).

Many cafés serve quick, tasty dishes

Kamiya Bar (beer hall and
restaurant) 1–1–1, Asakusa,
Taitō-ku (tel: (03) 3841-5400).
Matsuyoshi (general Japanese)
1–18–10, Nezu, Bunkyō-ku (tel:
(03) 3821-4430).
Morinaga (Western) 1–3–5,
Asakusa, Taitō-ku (tel: (03) 3841-
0558).
Roppongi Jack and Betty Club
(coffee-shop) 3–14–12, Roppongi,
Minato-ku (tel: (03) 3470-5650).
Shabutsuu (shabu-shabu)
3–17–2, Shinjuku, Shinjuku-ku
(tel: (03) 3354-2836).
Shakey's (fast food and pizza)
3–18–2, Shinjuku, Shinjuku-ku
(tel: (03) 3352-7473).
Shakey's (fast food and pizza)
3–9–10, Akasaka, Minato-ku (tel:
(03) 3582-4034).
**Shibuya Kinro-Fukushi-Kaikan
Shokudo** (general Japanese)
1–19–8, Jinnan, Shibuya-ku (tel:

(03) 3464-0158).
Shinjuku Jack and Betty Club
(coffee-shop) 3–24–3, Shinjuku,
Shinjuku-ku (tel: (03) 3350-0826).
Tatsumiya (general Japanese)
1–33–5, Asakusa, Taitō-ku (tel:
(03) 3842-7373).
Uchida (sushi) 2–8–15, Ginza,
Chūō-ku (tel: (03) 3564-2453).
Usagiya (Japanese/noodle)
3–41–1, Yushima, Bunkyō-ku tel:
(03) 3834-5800).
Usagiya (noodle) 5–9–18, Ginza,
Chūō-ku (tel: (03) 3573-5800).
Yoshinoya (general Japanese)
2–9–18, Yūrakuchō, Chiyoda-ku
(tel: (03) 3214-3660). Open 24
hours all through the year.

Shopping
Tōkyō is every shopper's
dream, not only for the amazing
range of goods available but
also for the quality of the
service. White-gloved, kimono-
clad ladies welcome you into
the better shops and
department stores. Inside, the
assistants are polite, helpful and
will wrap even the smallest
purchase as though it was a
precious stone. The best known
department stores include:
Mitsukoshi, which has its own
subway station; **Seibu**, one of
the most innovative and modern
stores, especially visit the
separate hardware section
called 'Loft' and the basement
food hall; **Wako**, an exclusive
and expensive shop (with an
amazing range of watches),
better known to the hoi polloi for
its pre-war clock tower, a
favourite meeting-place for
couples; and **Takashimaya**, the
flagship of Tōkyō's *depāto*
(department stores), opulent
décor matches their vast array

of famous fashion-named goods.
All these stores are located in
the Ginza district and are within
walking distance of one another.
Other shops to visit are the
fashion buildings (several floors
of fashion boutiques,
restaurants, bars and so on):
Axis in Roppongi, **Parco** in
Shibuya, and **La Foret** in
Harajuku (for everything a
teenager may wish to buy).
Tokyu Hands in the Shibuya
district is the most amazing DIY
shop in the world. There are
said to be over 3 million
different items for sale. **Wave** in
Roppongi is a 'concept retailing
outlet'. Several floors of audio
and visual software, eg video
tapes and discs, compact discs,
music cassettes, records, sheet
music and books. Japan is a
world leader in electronic
goods, but they are not cheaper
in Tōkyō than elsewhere. In fact,
they are often more expensive.
There is, however, an incredible
variety of goods on offer and
often the latest models and other
new, innovative equipment are
in the showrooms for sale
several months earlier than
anywhere else in the world.
There is no need to recommend
any particular store, one simply
goes to Akihabara Subway
Station, walks out of the station
and chooses a shop. Remember
to ask for an export model as
Japanese voltage is 100 volts.
Compare prices in several
shops before making a
purchase. The prices of clothes
by famous Japanese fashion
designers are around a third
less than in London and New
York, but sometimes they do not
stock Western sizes.

KAMAKURA

In the 12th century the military leader of Japan, Yoritomo Minamoto, moved the seat of military government away from Kyōto, where he believed the influence of the court was detrimental to the fighting spirit of his generals and their warriors. He chose to move to the isolated village of Kamakura, and established there Japan's first shogun-controlled military government. Over the next two centuries a number of Japan's most important temples and shrines were built there. The military and the clergy influenced one another to create a new breed of Zen warriors and warrior monks.

Nowadays, Kamakura, about one hour by train from Tōkyō, is one of the most interesting places in Japan for its historical temples and shrines. It is also an attractive and prosperous residential town in its own right. It is much smaller than Kyōto, Japan's other religious centre, and easier to find one's way around in. The local tourist information office publishes a convenient map of footpath routes that link the best-known temples. The paths are signposted in English as well as Japanese.

JR's Yokosuka Line connects Tōkyō to Kamakura. Trains are painted blue with white stripes and run about every 10 to 15 minutes. The train stops at Tōkyō, Shimbashi and Shinagawa stations on Tōkyō's Yamanote loop line. A more interesting route but a little longer is to take the Odakyu Line from Tōkyō to Fujisawa and change there to

Kamakura: a place of contemplation

catch a train on the Enoden narrow-gauge railway to Kamakura. The small train pulls three old wooden carriages and the journey is a delightful one through small villages. The line ends at Kamakura Station but *en route* passes Hase Station, the location of the Great Buddha and Hasedera Temple. Either station is a good starting point for a day walking tour, the best way to explore Kamakura. As an alternative, there is a good taxi service and distances are short. Kamakura provides a taste of old Japan.

WHAT TO SEE

There are many temples and shrines to visit in Kamakura but if time is limited the following are some of the most interesting.

◆◆◆
ENGAKUJI TEMPLE

Engakuji Temple was built in the 13th century by the Zen warrior Tokimune Hojo to commemorate the deaths of both Japanese and Mongolian soldiers killed during the Mongol's attempted invasion of Japan, and to mark his gratitude to Zen for the calm it had given him during the campaign. Engakuji has extensive gardens and grounds and numerous sub-temples, but perhaps **Shariden**, the Shrine of the Sacred Tooth of the Buddha, is the most interesting to visit. It is built in the Chinese style popular during the Kamakura era (1192–1333).
Open: 08.00–16.00 hrs, summer 08.00–17.00 hrs

◆◆◆
GREAT BUDDHA SHRINE

In the grounds of the Kotokuin Temple there is a bronze figure of a seated Buddha, the Daibutsu, over 35 feet (10m) in height. It was cast in the 13th century and at the time was housed in a massive wooden temple building. One hundred and forty years later the temple and Kamakura were flattened by a huge tidal wave that swept inland. The structure that housed the Buddha was swept away, but the Buddha itself remained unmoved and for the last six centuries it has stood in the open.
Open: 07.00–17.45 hrs

◆◆◆
KENCHOJI TEMPLE

Kenchoji, founded in 1253 as a training monastery for Zen monks, is the most important and most picturesque of Kamakura's Zen temples. There are few of over 50 original temple buildings still standing, and even these are reconstructions, but they do give some hint of the size of this complex in its heyday. There are elegant Zen gardens to explore and many paths to wander along in the surrounding pine forests.
Open: 09.30–16.30 hrs

◆◆◆
KOMYOJI TEMPLE

This temple is not on the usual tourist route, but is well worth a visit for the beautiful rock and gravel and lotus-pond gardens.
Open: 08.30–16.30 hrs

◆◆◆
TSURUGAOKA HACHIMANGU SHRINE

Hachiman is the god of war, and this shrine was originally built in the 12th century by members of the Minamoto clan, the foremost warrior clan of the time. It sits on a hillside overlooking the sea and the city. Near the front entrance to the temple is the **Kamakura Museum**, which houses art treasures from the 12th to 16th centuries.
Open: Shrine, 24 hours. Museum, Tuesday to Sunday 09.00–16.00 hrs

◆◆◆
ZENIARAI BENTEN SHRINE

This is called the Money-Washing Temple. The shrine is reached through a stone tunnel cut into a steep rock face. Once inside the temple grounds, one passes through a guard of honour of *torii* gates. They are erected so close together that they almost form a tunnel.

Off the main temple is a cave into which flows a mountain spring. The spring is directed into a channel that runs around the walls of the cave. Here is where the money-washing takes place. You put several coins in a wicker basket, swirl them under the water and wish for financial success.

Open: 07.00–17.45 hrs

Accommodation

Kamakura is so close to Tōkyō that relatively few people stay overnight. There are no very exclusive hotels, and those there are tend to be Japanese in style. Room charges usually include dinner and breakfast.

Kamakura Hotel, 2–22–29, Hase (tel: (0467) 22-0029). A one-minute walk from Hase Station. English spoken.

Tsurugaoka Kaikan Hotel, 2–2–27, Komachi (tel: (0467) 24-1111). A three-minute walk from Kamakura Station.

Restaurants

There are many places to eat and snack in and around Kamakura. The places listed are well known for specialising in particular dishes. If you wish to visit any of them ask at the counter at the tourist information office for one of the assistants to write the name in Japanese and show this to your taxi driver.

Fudo chaya (tel: (0467) 22-7839). A quaint tea-house selling noodles and Japanese sweets.

Hachinoki (tel: (0467) 22-8719). Zen vegetarian food.

Isomi-tei (tel: (0467) 24-9127)

(*soba*). Famous for its Japanese atmosphere.

Tori-ichi (tel: (0467) 22-1818) (chicken dishes). An attractive setting.

Shopping

Kamakura-bori or finely chiselled wood is the speciality of the area. Once finished the item, such as a jewellery box, is painted, usually red and black, and then lacquered to a glossy finish. There are many shops in Wakamiya Oji, the main street, and smaller surrounding streets selling *Kamakura-bori* as well as other craftware, antiques and gifts. For an unusual present try one of the shops selling religious artefacts for use in Zen temple ceremonies. The bells and gongs make a realistic sound.

The delicate art of **Kamakura-bori**

FUJI-HAKONE-IZU

The Fuji-Hakone-Izu National Park is the most popular excursion destination for residents of Tōkyō and throughout the spring and summer the area is busy with visitors. Outside these times it is relatively quiet since the Japanese operate in a very collective manner. The crater lakes, cone-shaped mountains and hot springs of Hakone, Fuji-san (Mount Fuji) and Izu-hantō (the Izu Peninsula) are the result of violent volcanic activity, some of it quite recent. The original wildness of the habitat has to some extent been sacrificed to the needs of tourists but the area is still beautiful. Indeed the Japanese believe that the symmetrical reflection of Fuji-san in the calm surface of Ashino-ko (Lake Ashi) to the southeast to be *the* most beautiful sight in the world.

HAKONE

Fuji-Hakone-Izu National Park is an area of high mountains (most over 4,000 feet/1,220m) with Lake Ashi nestling in the centre and Fuji-san (12,388 feet/3,776m) nearly always in view to the northwest. There are a number of hot-spring resorts for overnight stays, otherwise the best way to visit the area is to spend a full day travelling from Odawara, on the coast, into Hakone, around and back to Odawara. The Odakyu (private) Railway operates a frequent service from Shinjuku Station in Tōkyō to Odawara. The journey takes about 1 hour and 10 minutes. Odawara is also the

Fuji-san's snow-capped slopes

second stop from Tōkyō on the 'Kodama' Shinkansen train (not from 'Hikari'), and takes about 40 minutes.

Accommodation
Hotels and *ryokans* (inns) are expensive in this area and in season need to be booked ahead.

Hotels
Fujiya Hotel, 359, Miyanoshita, Hakone-machi (tel: (0460) 2-2211). Has an old library and a charming atmosphere.
Hakone Prince Hotel, 144, Moto-Hakone, Hakone-machi (tel: (0460) 3-7111). Good location. Two Japanese-style annexes.

Ryokans
Naraya, 162, Miyanoshita, Hakone-machi (tel: (0460) 2-2411). Elegant and formal, with lots of atmosphere. Family owned.

◆◆◆
FUJI-SAN ✓

The climbing season for Fuji-san 12,388 feet (3,776m) is 1 July to 31 August. It is a very long and steep walk rather than a climb. Nevertheless, it is arduous and should not be undertaken lightly. The mountain is a holy site for followers of Shinto and Buddhism, and many of those making the ascent will be pilgrims. All climbers hope to witness a sunrise from the top. This means either climbing overnight, a good choice but not recommended to the inexperienced walker, or climbing near to the top during the day, spending the night at the seventh or eighth stage in a crowded mountain hut, and then completing the ascent before sunrise. At close quarters the mountain is not beautiful. The rock is black and volcanic and there is no vegetation. Only the view from it lifts the spirits. Of course, if you are lucky enough to see a clear sunrise it is all worthwhile. The Japanese say that to climb Fuji-san once is wise but to climb it twice is foolish. Refreshments are available *en route*, but they are very expensive. Carry your own if you are poor and fit; if you can afford it, leave the weight behind and use the facilities available. Warm clothing is absolutely vital. If you do plan to climb Fuji-san plan it carefully and do not underestimate the severity of the climb even though you will see 70-year-old grandmothers (with full backpacks) at the base stations. Finally, it is worth noting that experienced guides have suggested that the best views of the sunrise are not from the top but from the eighth station (Hachigome).

How to Get There
For general sightseeing without planning an actual ascent on Fuji-san, Kawaguchiko is the centre of the area. To get to Kawaguchiko from Tōkyō you take a limited express train on the JR Chūō Line from Shinjuku Station, Tōkyō, change at Otsuki (1 hour) and then take a train on the private Fuji Kyuko Line to Kawaguchiko (50 minutes). Near the station there is a cable-car to the top of Mount Tenjozan, 3,622 feet (1,105m), from where magnificent views of Fuji-san are possible. From Kawaguchiko

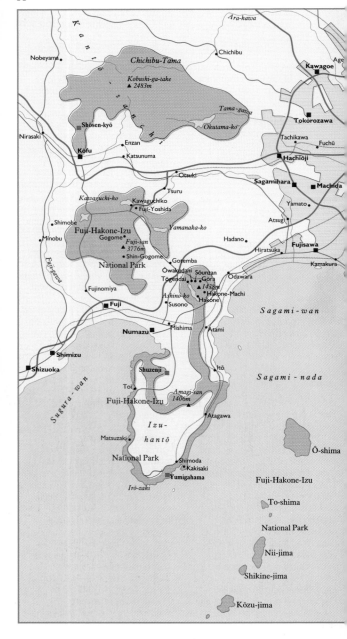

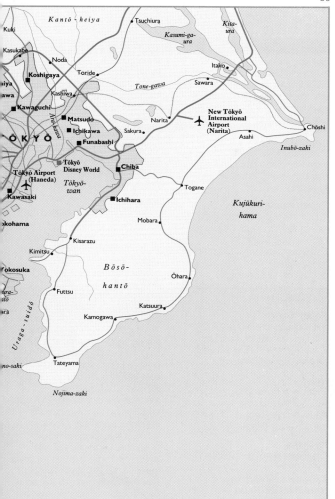

Kuki

Kasukabe

Noda

Koshigaya

iya

Toride

Kashiwa

Kawaguchi

TŌKYŌ

Matsudo

Ichikawa

Sakura

Funabashi

Tone-gawa

Kantō - heiya

Tsuchiura

Kasumi-ga-ura

Kita-ura

Itako

Sawara

Narita

New Tōkyō International Airport (Narita)

Asahi

Inubō-zaki

Chōshi

Tōkyō Disney World

Chiba

Togane

Kujūkuri-hama

Tōkyō Airport (Haneda)

Tōkyō-wan

Kawasaki

Ichihara

okohama

Mobara

okosuka

Kisarazu

Bōsō-hantō

Ōhara

ura-uidō

ura

Uraga-suidō

Kimitsu

Futtsu

Katsuura

Kamogawa

no-saki

Tateyama

Nojima-zaki

TŌKYŌ ENVIRONS, FUJI-SAN AND THE IZU PENINSULA

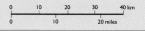

0   10   20   30   40 km

0   10   20 miles

Station there is a regular and frequent bus service to Gogome (55 minutes), the fifth stage on the route up Fuji-san and a regular starting-point for the climb. The service runs until late into the evening if you wish to make an overnight ascent.

There is also a direct bus service from Hamamatsucho or Shinjuku Bus Terminals, Tōkyō to Gogome (3 hours).

Accommodation

There are about 25 mountain huts above the fifth stage (fifth to the ninth stage) along the Kawaguchiko Trail and 11 along the Mishima-guchi Trail. Open from 1 July to 31 August. *Note*: Camping on the mountain is prohibited by law.

Youth Hostels

YH Kawaguchiko (tel: (0555) 72-1431). Five minute walk from Kawaguchiko Station. Closed November to late March.

Hotel

Fuji View Hotel (tel: (0555) 83-2211). Five minutes by car from Kawaguchiko Station. (Tōkyō office: (03) 3573-3911).

Ryokans

Fuji Lake Hotel (tel: (0555) 72-2209). Four minutes by car from Kawaguchiko Station.
Kawaguchiko Hotel (tel: (0555) 72-1313). Five minutes by car from Kawaguchiko Station.
Hotel Kogetsukan (tel: (0555) 72-1180). Three minutes by car from Kawaguchiko Station.
Hotel Mifujien (tel: (0555) 72-1044). Ten minutes by bus from Kawaguchiko Station.
Yamagishi Ryokan (tel: (0555) 72-2218). Eight minutes on foot from Kawaguchiko Station.

Minshuku

Hotel Ashiwada (tel: (0555) 82-2321). Fifteen minutes by car from Kawaguchiko Station. Get off at Nagahama bus stop.

Pension

Pension People (tel: (0555) 76-6069). Twenty minutes by bus from Kawaguchiko Station. Get off at Oishi-Petit-Pension Mura bus stop.

◆◆◆
IZU-HANTO (IZU-PENINSULA)

Izu-hanto, which juts out from the mainland into the Pacific Ocean, is an area with a number of hot-spring resorts both along its coastline and in the interior. It is only about one hour from Tōkyō to Atami, at the northern end of the peninsula, and Izu is a popular resort with residents of Tōkyō . Atami is a large, rather vulgar holiday town and worth only a short stop before proceeding down the scenic east-coast road to Itō and then Shimoda. Regular bus and train services operate between Atami and Shimoda. From Shimoda there is a bus route (2 hours) through the mountainous interior to Shuzenji, a traditional and rather prestigious spa town, from where a direct train to Tōkyō (2 hours, 40 minutes) can be taken. South of Shimoda is the lovely Yumigahama Beach and Cape Iro, a cliff-top town with a 'Jungle Garden' (fascinating place, rather shabby setting).

◆◆◆
ITŌ

Itō is where Will Adams, the English ship's pilot who inspired the novel *Shogun*, lived. Near the town harbourmaster's office there

Itō spa: the town has 700 hot springs

is a memorial stone to him. The wording in English and Japanese celebrates his amazing exploits.

William Adams was born in Kent in 1564. At the age of 12 he was apprenticed to a shipyard, where he studied astronomy and navigation as well as shipbuilding. In 1598 he set out from Holland as chief pilot of a fleet of five vessels heading for the Orient. After a long voyage his ship was caught in a gale and washed ashore off the coast of Kyūshū. He was taken to Osaka castle, where he was held for many days before being interrogated by Shogun Tokugawa Ieyasu himself. The shogun was impressed by Adams and his knowledge of navigation and shipbuilding. He appointed him to the post of adviser on foreign affairs and installed him in a house in Edo (now Tōkyō).

In 1604 the shogun ordered Adams to build an 80-ton Western-style sailing ship. The construction work was carried out on the estuary of the Matsa-Kawa River in Itō. The shogun was pleased with the boat and ordered Adams to build an ocean-going vessel. This later underwent successful sea trials. For some reason the shogun loaned it to a Spanish diplomat who sailed the ship to Acapulco, Mexico. It was never returned to Japan.

Adams was rewarded for his services to the shogunate with a large estate. He was given the status of a samurai, and the two swords he was allowed to carry were given by the shogun himself. He adopted the Japanese name Miura Anjin and married a Japanese woman called Yuki. Anjin and his wife had two children. He continued his life as a pilot and died in Japan of natural causes aged 56.

FUJI-HAKONE-IZU

Music-makers in Kyōto

◆◆◆
SHIMODA

Shimoda has an important place in Japanese history since it was here in 1854 that the first important trade treaty between America and Japan was signed. Japan was bullied into ending over 200 years of self-imposed isolation by Commodore Perry and his 12 black warships. Three years after the signing of the treaty Townsend Harris took up residence in a village near Shimoda. He was the first American consul to Japan and his supposed affair with a Japanese girl was possibly the model for Puccini's opera, *Madame Butterfly*.

Ryosen-ji is the temple where the treaty was signed. Among the Japanese, however, Ryosen-ji is better known as the home of a collection of explicit erotic art. The temple authorities describe the exhibits as 'Buddhist images symbolising ecstasy'. (*Open*: 08.30–17.00 hrs.)

The village of **Kakisaki** is 30 minutes' walk along the coast from Shimoda. This is where Harris set up his consulate. It has now been converted into a Shinto temple with a cemetery on one side. It is a cosy, very Japanese place off the tourist-coach circuit.

Accommodation

The Izu Peninsula has many hotels, *ryokans* and *onsen minshuku*, a sort of hot-spring bed and breakfast where your room is in a large family-style house fitted with a large public bath fed by underground hot springs. This type of lodging is both the cheapest and most interesting. All the main towns on the peninsula have tourist information offices where the assistants will help you find and book accommodation.

SOUTH CENTRAL JAPAN (KANSAI DISTRICT)

Until the Meiji Restoration in 1868 this region was the heart of Japan, culturally, politically and economically. It is still of great importance, being the region of Kyōto, the nation's spiritual home; Osaka, the industrial and commercial centre of the country; and Nara, the first capital of Japan. More information may be obtained on these at the Tourist Information Centre (TIC) in Kyōto Tower, Kyōto (tel: (075) 371-5649; closed Saturday afternoon and Sunday). You can also pick up a copy of the free monthly English-language Kyōto guide.

KYŌTO

Kyōto is the religious capital of Japan and, until the end of the Edo period in 1868, the home for many centuries of the imperial family. It is a lovely city of temples, Zen gardens and Shinto shrines, and in the quiet back streets of the old quarters, craft shops, traditional houses and Japanese inns. Do not be put off by first impressions, the area around the railway station is faceless and modern and not representative of much of the city. Kyōto is a magnet for tourists, both Japanese and foreign, but there is so much to see and do that crowds only form at the most popular places. Avoid the city on public holidays and the best known temples at weekends to avoid the crowds. Almost opposite the main entrance of Kyōto Station, across a wide busy road, is the TIC office.

Kyōto Tower is a modern landmark

Here you can obtain free street and railway maps of Kyōto and, if you need to, enquire about accommodation. The city feels small, but if you are walking it takes a long time going between the different sites of interest, so do not plan to do too much. If you are short of time take a taxi. A good way to get about Kyōto is by bicycle, and there are several cycle shops in the city where bicycles can be hired by the day. **Nippon Rent-a-Car** opposite the Hachijo exit of Kyōto Station (tel: (075) 622-3045); **Rent-a-Cycle Heian** on the west side of the Imperial Palace (tel: (075) 431-4522); **Rent-a-Cycle Yasamoto** near Keihan-Sanjo Station (tel: (075) 751-0595).

KYŌTO

0   ½   1   1½   2 km
0   ½   1 mile

OMIYA

Kita - ku

KITAYAMA - DORI

SHICHIKU

HORIKAWA - DORI

KOYA

Daitokuji Temple

MURASAKINO

KITAOJI - DORI

Kinkakuji Temple

KINUGASA

RYOANJI

Ryoanji Temple

Zen Garden

KITSUJI-DORI

Kitano Temmangu Shrine

NISHIOJI-DORI

IMADEGAWA-DORI

UTANO

NISHIJIN

OMURO

Myoshinji Temple

TAISHOGUN

SEMBON-DORI

Kamigyo - ku

MARUTAMACHI-DORI

JR SAN-IN

Omuro-gawa

Tenjin - gawa

NISHINOKYO

Nijo Castle

UZUMASA

OIKE-DORI

OIKE - DORI

SANJO-DORI

YAMANOUCHI

Nakagyo - ku

HORIKAWA-DORI

SHIJO-DORI

Mibu Temple

NISHI-OHASHI BRIDGE

NISHIOJI-DORI

MIBU

OMIYA-DORI

NISHI-GOJO-DORI

Yusen Cultural Hall

Shimogyo - k

Nishi-Honganji Temple

Katsura-gawa

SUZAKU

SHICHIJO-DORI

NISHI-KYOGOKU

HACHIJO-DORI

UMEKOJI

KATSURA-OHASHI BRIDGE

KARAHASHI

Toji Temple

Minami-ku

KUJO-DORI

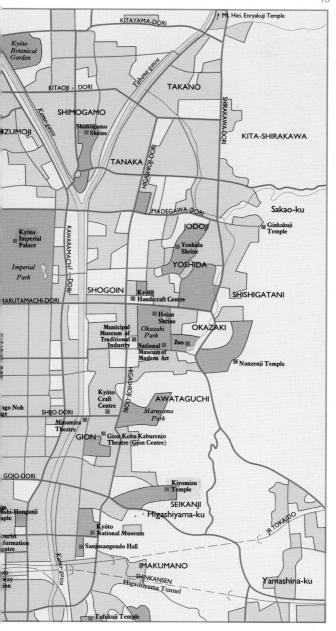

KITAYAMA-DORI

↑ Mt. Hiei, Enryakuji Temple

Kyōto Botanical Garden

KITAOJI - DORI

TAKANO

SHIMOGAMO

IZUMOJI

Shimogamo Shrine

KITA-SHIRAKAWA

TANAKA

IMADEGAWA-DORI

Sakao-ku

JODOJI

Ginkakuji Temple

Kyōto Imperial Palace

Yoshida Shrine

YOSHIDA

Imperial Park

SHOGOIN

Kyōto Handicraft Centre

SHISHIGATANI

MARUTAMACHI-DORI

Heian Shrine

Municipal Museum of Traditional Industry

Okazaki Park

OKAZAKI

National Museum of Modern Art

Zoo

Nanzenji Temple

Kyōto Craft Centre

AWATAGUCHI

Maruyama Park

ngo Noh ge

SHIJO-DORI

Minamiza Theatre

GION

Gion Kobu Kaburenjo Theatre (Gion Centre)

GOJO-DORI

Kiyomizu Temple

SEIKANJI

shi-Honganji ple

Higashiyama-ku

Kyōto National Museum

urist formation ntre

Sanjusangendo Hall

to way on

IMAKUMANO

JR TOKAIDO

SHINKANSEN

Higashiyama Tunnel

Yamashina-ku

Tofukuji Temple

SOUTH CENTRAL JAPAN

WHAT TO SEE

◆◆◆
DAITOKUJI TEMPLE
northwestern Kyōto

A Rinzai Zen monastery and a centre of the tea ceremony. There are 24 separate temples, of which 8 are open to the public. The gardens, buildings and their contents are exquisite examples of the elegance and beauty of Zen architecture and art. One of the most beautiful Zen gardens in Kyōto, and possibly the least visited, is that of the **Koto-In Temple**, a small sub-temple of Daitokuji that has only three buildings and a garden.
Open: 09.00–16.30 hrs. The main grounds of Daitokuji sub-temples are always open. *Buses*: 1, 12, 61, 204, 205, 206.

◆◆◆
GINKAKUJI TEMPLE (SILVER PAVILION)

eastern Kyōto

The Silver Pavilion was built in 1489 by the Shogun Yoshimasa Ashikaga. The main plans for the temple were inspired by the design of the Golden Pavilion (see page 47) built by Yoshimasa's grandfather, Shogun Yoshimitsu Ashikaga. He planned to cover the entire structure with silver foil, but died before this could be started. However, the Silver Pavilion is still perhaps the most interesting of the two. Yoshimasa was an aesthete who had a special interest in the arts, and he included in the temple buildings rooms designed especially for pastimes such as flower viewing, moon watching, the tea ceremony, incense smelling and poetry composition.

The garden of this temple which was originally built as a country house, is a delightfully formal affair with the requisite arranged mosses, rocks, pond and sand mountains.

The Silver Pavilion is connected to the classic Zen temple, **Nanzenji**, by a quiet canal-side towpath known as The Path of Philosophy (take bus no 5 to Ginkakuji-michi, then a 50-minute walk). There are a number of coffee-shops and restaurants along the way. Nanzenji is worth visiting for a little peace and tranquillity after the busyness of Ginkakuji.
Open: 08.30–17.00 hrs; 1 December to 14 March 09.00–16.30 hrs
Buses: 5, 17, 203

◆◆
HEIAN SHRINE
eastern Kyōto

This vast, vermilion-coloured Shinto shrine is dedicated to the emperors Kammu and Komei, the first and last to reign in Kyōto. The shrine is a rather gaudy affair, but it is popular with the citizens of Kyōto and is the centre of a number of festivals.
Heian Shrine is also the focal point for Okazaki Park, an area of museums, Kyōto Zoo and a concert hall. The **National Museum of Modern Art** has a fine collection of contemporary ceramics (*open*: Tuesday to Sunday 09.30–17.00 hrs). The **Municipal Museum of Traditional Industry** displays and sells Kyōto crafts (*open*: 09.00–17.00 hrs). It also has a replica of an old Kyōto home (*open*: 13.00–16.30 hrs). **Kyōto Zoo** has a children's

corner (*open*: 09.00–17.00 hrs, December to February 09.00–16.30 hrs; closed Mondays). Behind the shrine is a Chinese-style 'pond-garden', famous for its water-lilies.
Open: Garden, 08.30–17.00 hrs; winter 08.30–16.30 hrs
Buses: 5, 2, 3

◆◆◆ KINKAKUJI TEMPLE (GOLDEN PAVILION) ✓

northwestern Kyōto
Built in 1397 for the third Ashikaga-era shogun, Yoshimitsu, as a country retreat for his retirement from politics. The dome is covered in gold leaf. It reflects perfectly in the calm water of the pond that lies in front of it. The temple was deliberately burned down in 1950 by a priest. It was rebuilt in 1955.

Reflected gold in Kinkakuji Temple

Open: 09.00–17.30 hrs; October to March 09.00–17.00 hrs
Buses: 59, 204, 205
Southwest of the temple and closeby is the famous Zen Garden of **Ryoanji Temple** (see page 48).

◆◆ MOUNT HIEI AND ENRYAKUJI TEMPLE

northeastern Kyōto
To the northeast of Kyōto is the steep sided Mount Hiei, 2,790 feet (850m). Mount Hiei is mentioned frequently in Japanese Buddhist literature since for 12 centuries it has been the site of Enryakuji, at one time the most influential Buddhist monastery in Japan. Nowadays there is a cable-car almost to the summit. From the top footpaths lead down to the temple complex.
The principal temple buildings are collected in two areas, known as the eastern and western precincts. The eastern precinct is

Shops light the way in Kyōto

more easily reached by tourist coaches. The western precincts are less visited and the best areas for good walkers.
Open: 08.30–16.30 hrs; December to March 09.00–16.00 hrs
Bus: Express bus from Kyōto Station to Yaseyuen Station. Cable-car from Yaseyuen up Mount Hiei, then a 40-minute walk.

◆◆◆
RYOANJI TEMPLE ZEN GARDEN
northwestern Kyōto
Ryoanji is near the Golden Pavilion, and it is worth visiting both on the same trip. The Zen Garden is always busy.
There are three basic types of Japanese garden: the tea garden is usually designed by tea-masters as a site for the tea ceremony; the hill garden, designed for private estates, is a small park with miniature artificial hills; and the flat garden. The Zen

Garden at Ryoanji is an extreme version of the flat garden. In this style, the most common elements are stones, sand and gravel. The garden was created by Soami, a famous ink-line artist. It consists only of raked gravel and 15 rocks, and certainly obeys the injunction written by an anonymous 16th-century painter and gardener: 'Caution should be taken not to be too anxious to overcrowd the scenery to make it more interesting. Such an effect often results in a loss of dignity and a feeling of vulgarity.'
Open: 08.00–17.00 hrs; December to February 08.30–16.30 hrs
Bus: 59

◆◆◆
NIJO CASTLE
central Kyōto
Built in 1603 as a residence for the shogun, Ieyasu Tokugawa, it has a moat, turrets and a massive

entrance gate, but inside it is not like a castle. Most visitors go to see the lavish and ornate audience halls designed to impress or humble friends or enemies. Its specially constructed 'nightingale' floor warns of approaching visitors.
Open: 08.45–16.00 hrs. Tours in English.
Subway station: Oike
Buses: 9, 12, 50, 61

◆◆
SANJUSANGENDO HALL
eastern Kyōto
The popular name of Renegeoin Temple, it refers to the 33 (*sanjusan*) spaces between the pillars that support the roof of this very long but narrow hall. Its main image is a wooden statue of a seated, thousand-armed Kannon (Buddhist saint of compassion). This is surrounded by 1,000 smaller standing Kannon images, each with a different face. Together they represent the infinite compassion of Kannon. Sanjusangendo Hall is famous for the archery contests that have been held there since the Edo period. They take place in January and May, and Japan's top archers take part.
Open: Mid-March to October 08.00–17.00 hrs; November to mid-March 08.00–16.00 hrs
Buses: 206, 208

Accommodation
There are many hotels and *ryokans* in Kyōto, but during spring and autumn and over public holidays they are heavily booked. The *ryokans* in Kyōto tend to be very good. For very cheap accommodation, probably in a room with people of several different nationalities, **Tani**

House, 8 Daitokuji-cho, Murasakino, Kita-ku, Kyōto (tel: (075) 492-5489), is the place. It is run by a relaxed and friendly Japanese couple who speak some English. It is also very near **Koto-In**, a very beautiful Zen garden (see under **Daitokuji Temple**, page 46). In a real emergency you can usually be 'squeezed in'.

Luxury-class Hotels
Miyako Hotel, Sanjo-Keage, Higashiyama-ku, Kyōto (tel: (075) 771-7111). Has a Japanese wing. Good service.
Takaragaike Prince Hotel, Takaragaikè, Sakao-ku, Kyōto (tel: (075) 712-1111). Large rooms with good views of the mountains and forests. It has a beautifully constructed tea-house.

Ryokans
Hiiragiya Ryokan, Aneyakoji North, Fuyacho, Nakagyo-ku, Kyōto (tel: (075) 221-1136).
Sumiya Ryokan, Sanjo South, Fuyacho-dori, Nakagyo-ku, Kyōto (tel: (075) 221-2187).
Yachiyo, 34, Nanzenji-Fukuchicho, Sakyo-ku, Kyōto (tel: (075) 771-4148).

First-class Hotel
International Hotel Kyōto, 284, Nijo-Aburankoji, Nakagyo-ku, Kyōto (tel: (075) 222-1111). One of Kyōto's best hotels. English-speaking staff.

Tourist Hotels
Hotel Gimmond, Takakura, Oike-dori, Nakagyo-ku, Kyōto (tel: (075) 221-4111). English-speaking staff.
Holiday Inn Kyōto, 36, Nishihirakicho, Takano, Sakyo-ku, Kyōto (tel: (075) 721-3131). Good sports facilities.

Kyōto Palaceside Hotel,
Shimodachiuri-agaru, Karasuma-
dori, Kamigyo-ku, Kyōto (tel:
(075) 431-8171). Near the old
Imperial Palace.

Inexpensive Ryokan

Hiraiwa Ryokan, 314, Hayaocho,
Kaminoguchiagaru, Ninomiya-
dori, Shimogyou-ku, Kyōto (tel:
(075) 351-6748). Comfortable
and friendly. English-speaking
staff.

Entertainment

Kyōto is not noted for its nightlife,
nor does it aspire to be. There
are cultural events throughout the
year and traditional entertainment
such as Noh theatre. See
**Culture, Entertainment and
Nightlife** (pages 100–1) for
general comments and listings of
Kyōto cultural centres.

Restaurants

The cuisine of Kyōto is derived
from that of the court of the
imperial family, and it is the most
refined of all styles of Japanese
cooking. Zen vegetarian dishes,
tofu dishes and traditional *kaiseki*
tea-ceremony food are
especially recommended. There
are many restaurants in town,
and the TIC office publishes a
Kyōto Gourmet Guide, which is
worth picking up.
The following is a small selection
of better-known city-centre
establishments.
Ebisugawa-tei (tel: (075) 222-
1511) (steakhouse).
Kanoko (tel: (075) 351-2081)
(shabu-shabu).
Kimura Sukiyaki-ten (tel: (075)
221-0506) (sukiyaki).
Kitamura (tel: (075) 351-7871)
(kaiseki). Traditional Kyōto
cooking.

Maruman Sushi (tel: (075) 221-
0927) (sushi).
Okina-tei (tel: (075) 221-0250).
The oldest sukiyaki shop in Japan.
Owariya (tel: (075) 231-3446)
(soba).
Takesebune (tel: (075) 351-4032)
(sashimi). Atmospheric and value
for money.
Yamamoto (tel: (075) 231-4495)
(tonkatsu, or pork cutlet).

OSAKA

Osaka is connected to Tōkyō by
more than 100 express trains a
day, and international flight
connections between the two
cities are normally free. Prices
are a little lower and hotel
accommodation is easier to get
than in either Kyōto or Tōkyō. It
is an interesting city in its own right
and a convenient base for
exploring Kyōto, Nara and Kobe.
Osaka is Japan's major port and
centre of commerce. It has had a
reputation for being grimy,
chaotic and cramped. Some of
that description still holds true,
but it is a city of great energy and
the city fathers, with an eye to the
economic and sociological
importance of ecological issues,
are spending large sums of
money to improve the city
environment.
Osaka is not a tourist town nor
are there many places of scenic
or historic interest to visit, but for
a keyhole view of real Japanese
city life and the closest there is to
a working-class Japan, it should
not be missed.
The Japanese describe Osaka as
shominteki, a place of the people,
where appearance is less
important than substance and
where the citizens have no time

for pretensions. As one might expect, food is more important than fashion and the city is famous for its restaurants and cuisine. Osakans are known as *Kuidores,* those who eat to the point of physical and financial ruin. Restaurants of every type and price are found throughout the city and prices are low. Local specialities are the street food, *takoyaki,* a wheat flour dumpling stuffed with octopus meat and baked over charcoal; *udon,* fat white wheat noodles; and *Osaka-sushi,* squares of sticky sweet rice and raw fish. On the tenth floor of the Hanshin department store, which has three basement floors descending into the subterranean town beneath Osaka Station, there are a wide variety of restaurants where many types of local dishes can be ordered.

For shopping, in the **Umeda** area, locally called Kita, there is a maze of glass-covered pedestrian-only arcades lined with shops and restaurants. They open onto plazas with department stores and street markets. For nightlife **Dotonburi Street**, around Namba Station, is a hive of bars, coffee lounges and nightclubs illuminated by flashing neon and an open-air, 40-foot (12m) high video screen.

Osaka Castle is a massive construction and worth visiting, but the park which surrounds it is the best place in the city for watching people. The Japanese spend little time at home, and public places are busy seven days a week. They like to wear or use the best and latest equipment for whichever pastime they enjoy. Joggers in

Imposing Osaka Castle

pristine clean and pressed tracksuits plus apparently unused trainers slowly run through the park's plum and cherry tree orchards. The Shinkansen from Tōkyō takes between 2½ and 3 hours and arrives at Shin-Osaka Station. Change here and travel a few stops south on a loop line to Osaka Station in the centre of town. The Osaka street system and its subway are very complicated and it is easy to get lost under- or overground. Do not explore without a map and a copy of your accommodation address in Japanese.

Osaka's futuristic new Kansai International Airport opened in September 1994. It is located on an artificial island in Osaka Bay. There are connections from here to all main Japanese destinations and to over 40 countries worldwide.

The very best hotel in Osaka is the **New Otani**, a futuristic place which overlooks Osaka Castle, where the services and service are impeccable and prices are steep. The **Osaka Terminal Hotel** is right in the middle of town and actually within the Osaka Station complex. It is reasonable and very convenient if you are making a brief visit.

Hotel New Otani, 1–4–1, Shiromi Chuo-ku, Osaka (tel: (06) 941-1111).

Osaka Terminal Hotel, 3–1–1, Umeda, Kita-ku, Osaka (tel: (06) 344-1235).

NARA

Nara was the first political and cultural centre of a united Japan. However, the capital moved to Kyōto towards the end of the 8th century and Nara slowly lapsed into relative obscurity. This was a blessing in disguise as the city escaped much of the war damage suffered by other cities in Japan's long civil wars. As a result, Nara and the monastery estates around it contain some of the best examples of traditional Japanese architecture and art that can be seen today. The sights may be approximately divided into two areas: those in and around Nara Park, a large but not very attractive park well known for its 'wild' deer; and the southwest district of the city where several major temples are situated.

Nara is a famous historical city, but it tends to be a place that tourists visit on a day-only basis. This is because there is not a lot of accommodation and travel times between Nara and Kyōto or Osaka are short. The JR Nara Line connects Kyōto to Nara (1 hour), trains run once or twice an hour. The JR Kansai Honsen Line connects Osaka to Nara (50 minutes), trains run three times an hour.

A city map and walk route is available from the tourist information office in the Kintetsu-Nara Station (first floor).

WHAT TO SEE – NARA PARK AREA

◆◆
KASUGA TAISHA SHRINE
One of Japan's most famous shrines. Set in spacious wooded grounds, the temple buildings are made of vermilion lacquered wood and designated national treasures.
Open: 08.30–16.30 hrs; November to March 09.00–16.00 hrs

◆◆◆
KOFUKUJI TEMPLE
Constructed in 710 and once filled with 175 buildings, the temple is now famous for its five-storey pagoda built in 1426 as an exact replica of the 8th-century original.
Also, at **Sarusawanoike Pond** south of Kofukuji, a five-storey pagoda is reflected on the pond's surface. A popular spot for atmospheric photographs.
Open: 09.00–17.00 hrs

◆◆◆
NARA NATIONAL MUSEUM
An exhibition of ancient works of art, especially Buddhist-influenced images. Recommended, but particularly during the last week in October and first week in November when the treasures of Todaiji Temple are displayed.
Open: 09.00–16.30 hrs (closed Mondays)

SHIN-YAKUSHIJI TEMPLE

One original building, among later structures, from the 8th century and a well-known sculpture of the God of Medicine. It is surrounded by clay sculptures of the Twelve Divine Generals, renowned for their powerful expressions.
Open: 08.30–18.00 hrs

TODAIJI TEMPLE ✓

One of Japan's most beautiful monasteries. Home of the world's largest bronze statue of the Buddha (many temples in southeast Asia also make this claim for their own Buddha), and other sculptures and temple buildings of historical and cultural importance.
Open: March 08.00–17.00 hrs;

Todaiji Temple: symmetry and grace

April to September 07.30–17.30 hrs; October 07.30–17.00 hrs; November to February 08.00–16.00 hrs

WHAT TO SEE – SOUTHWEST NARA

CHUGUJI NUNNERY

A convent especially famous for its 7th-century wooden statue of Miroku-bosatsu, a female face of Kannon the Buddhist embodiment of compassion and mercy. Quiet and peaceful temple grounds.
Open: 09.00–16.15 hrs; 1 October to 20 March 09.00–15.45 hrs

HORYUJI TEMPLE

Horyuji is a little off the beaten track, but should not be missed. It was founded in 607 by Prince Shotoku, a great protector of the Buddhist faith. There are 40

buildings, all of them
designated as national
treasures. Some have been
claimed to be the oldest still-
standing wooden structures in
the world. Others were rebuilt
or added later.
Open: 08.30–16.30 hrs; 10
November to 10 March
08.00–16.00 hrs
Bus: from Kintetsu-Nara Station to
Horyuji (38 minutes)

◆◆◆
TOSHOSAIJI TEMPLE
A physically beautiful temple .
Erected in 759 by the Chinese
priest, Ganjin, at the invitation of
the Emperor. Toshosaiji has not
been damaged by fire,
earthquake or war and many of
the original buildings still stand.
The eight pillars at the front of
Kondo Hall show the influence of
Greek architecture,
demonstrating the influence of
the 'Silk Road' even at this early
time.

*You will find plenty of friendly faces
all over Japan*

Open: 08.30–16.30 hrs
Bus : from Kintetsu-Nara Station
to Toshosaiji

◆◆◆
YAKUSHIJI TEMPLE
An important repository of
Hakuko-period art and
architecture. It was founded in
680 and includes an unusual
three-storey pagoda, the only
building within the temple to
have remained unchanged. It is
connected to Toshaiji by a street
called the Path of History (10
minute walk), used over the
centuries by emperors and
nobles. An English-language
booklet, available at the entrance,
provides a guide to the temple
and to the art and architecture
collection.
Open: 08.30–16.30 hrs
Bus: from Kintetsu-Nara Station to
Horyuji

WESTERN JAPAN

This region, which includes the western end of Honshū and all of Shikoku, is an area of great contrasts both geographically and culturally.

San-in, which stretches along the northern coast of Western Honshū and faces the Japan Sea, is a rather isolated area often ignored by foreign tourists. It is, however, worth visiting for its coastal and mountain scenery and historic castle and spa towns. The San-yo coastal area on the southern coast of Honshū is a corridor of heavy residential development and industry. The Shinkansen express train line travels through San-yo. Hiroshima and Okayama are the main towns and Shinkansen station stops in this region.

Shikoku, which lies across the Setonaikai (Seto Inland Sea) opposite the San-yo coast, is the smallest of Japan's four main islands. It is one of the least explored regions of Japan, either by Japanese or foreign tourists.

SHIKOKU

For the Japanese, Shikoku is best known as the centre of Shingon Buddhism. Every year thousands of followers make a walking tour (and more recently bus tour) pilgrimage of the island's 88 Shingon temples in memory of the priest Kobo Daishi, founder of the sect. Many of the temples can arrange overnight accommodation and a tour of some of them would make an interesting trip. At the moment only Japanese maps of the route are available.

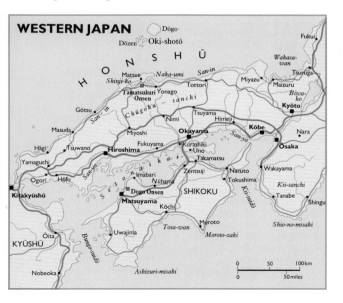

The interior of the island is mountainous and a place of remote hiking trails, clean rivers, Zen temples and tiny villages.

How To Get There

A direct train to Takamatsu leaves Tōkyō Station every night at 21.05 hrs, arriving at 07.35 hrs the following morning. There are regular services to Takamatsu from Okayama Station, Tōkyō, on the Shinkansen Line to Okayama (3 hours, 50 minutes) followed by a rapid train to Takamatsu (1 hour). JR ferry and hovercraft services connect Uno on Honshū to Takamatsu. Uno is connected to Okayama by a frequent tram service. Takamatsu is also connected by an air service to Osaka and Tōkyō.

Shikoku's three main railway lines begin at Takamatsu. They are: the JR Yosan Line to Matsuyama; the JR Dosan Line to Kochi; and the JR Kotoku Line to Tokushima. The tourist information office is at the station, but only supplies local information. Information on the whole island needs to be obtained in Tōkyō.

WHAT TO SEE

TAKAMATSU

A small, pleasant town and a convenient centre for exploring the rest of Shikoku. Ritsurin Park is the main tourist destination. After dark, Takamatsu has a busy night life and the 'entertainment area' is a maze of neon-lit, pedestrian-only arcades lined with bars, restaurants, strip joints and late-night shops.

RITSURIN PARK

Takamatsu was bombed flat in the war but fortunately Ritsurin-Kōen (Park) in the north of the city, famous even outside Shikoku, escaped damage. The South Garden of the park is of classical design and contains the requisite six ponds and thirteen hills.
Open: Park sunrise to sunset; Teahouse 08.30–16.00 hrs

ZENTSUJI TEMPLE

Zentsuji Temple, on the Dosan Line south of Takamatsu (40 minutes), is the birthplace of Kobo Daishi and the 75th station of the 88 temples. A statue of the saint guards the entrance to the temple.

MATSUYAMA

Shikoku's largest city, but with more of a country-town atmosphere than Takamatsu. The tourist information office is inside the station.

DOGO ONSEN (SPA)

Dogo Onsen is one of the best known and oldest hot-spring, public baths in Japan. A part of it, still preserved and open for viewing, was originally set aside for the exclusive use of visiting royalty from Kyōto. This area is ornate, but the section open for public bathing is simply designed and in the best tradition of functional Japanese architecture. A trolleybus line runs from just outside the railway station directly to Dogo Onsen (15 minutes). At the entrance to the baths one pays a fee according to services provided.
Open: 06.30–22.00 hrs

MATSUYAMA CASTLE

First built in 1630 and rebuilt in 1830, the castle sits high above the city. It covers an extensive area and many of the stone walls, turrets and the keep are in good condition. Feels like a 'real' castle.

Open: 09.00–17.00 hrs

UWAJIMA

Uwajima is the last stop on the railway line west from Takamatsu and a 5½ hour journey. Trains leave Takamatsu for Uwajima about five times daily. It is a small country town well known locally for its bullring (two bulls, like four-legged sumo wrestlers, each try to push the other out of a small ring). Outside the station is a small tourist information office. Taga Jinja is the local Shinto shrine. The priest there is also an avid collector of sexual memorabilia. He has built, adjacent to the shrine, a three-storey museum to house his collection.

Open: 08.00–17.00 hrs

SAN-YO

HIROSHIMA

Hiroshima has been an important town since early in Japanese history. The feudal lord Terumoto Mori built a castle on the present site of the city in the 16th century and named it Hiroshima Castle. From that time forwards the area had important military significance. During both world wars Hiroshima was a centre of weapons manufacture. On 6 August 1945, at 08.15 hrs, it was the target of the world's first atom bomb attack. The city was completely and instantly destroyed and 200,000 people died while 6,000 people a year still die from the after-effects. The city is now completely rebuilt and has a population of over one

Hiroshima, monument to war's atrocity

million. It is a successful manufacturing and commercial centre, but a tourist destination rather because of what happened than for its own sake. The Peace Memorial Park in Hiroshima contains a museum, monuments and other memories of the bomb. Hiroshima is a station on the main Shinkansen Line from Tōkyō to Hakata Station (Fukuoka). Tōkyō to Hiroshima: 5 hours. Kyōto to Hiroshima: 2 hours.

WHAT TO SEE

PEACE MEMORIAL PARK

The park is 15 minutes by tram or bus from the railway station. It is situated on a delta island in the Odagawa River. The museum and cenotaph were designed by a Japanese and the Peace Bridges by an American.
Open: 24 hours

Atomic Bomb Dome

A bomb-damaged building left standing as a sad symbol of the destructive power of the bomb.

The Cenotaph

Contains a roll call of the victims.

Peace Memorial Museum

Open: December to April 09.00–16.30 hrs; May to November 09.00–17.30 hrs
Closed: 29 December to 2 January

SAN-IN

There is much to see of ordinary Japanese life along the San-in coast, but nothing spectacular and the reason to go there is to enjoy a quiet, quite rural part of Japan not visited often by foreign tourists or catering for them. There are, however, three towns

worth stopping at: Matsue, Tsuwano and Hagi.

MATSUE

Matsue, the 'city of water', is situated between Nakaumi Lagoon and Lake Shinji. It is a pleasant but busy town, best known outside the region for being the home of Lafcadio Hearn, the 19th-century writer who wrote many popular books in English about his impressions and experiences in Japan. The Matsue of today would not be recognised by Hearn except for his house, which is preserved, and the castle near the walls of which the house stands. There are excellent *onsen* (hot springs) around Matsue and Tamatsukuri Onsen (30 minutes by bus from Matsue) is particularly recommended. To visit Matsue during the day and to spend the night at a lodging in Tamatsukuri Onsen would be a good plan.

WHAT TO SEE

KOIZUMI YAKUMO KYUKYO

Originally a samurai dwelling and then the home of Lafcadio Hearn (Koizumi Yakumo). Opposite the northern moat of the castle.
Open: 09.00–16.00 hrs
Closed: Wednesdays

MATSUE CASTLE

The original keep (the donjon) and some other stone fortifications still stand. The view from the top of the keep of the city and Shinji-ko (Lake Shinji) makes the climb worthwhile.
Open: 08.30–17.00 hrs
Bus: No 1 or 2 from Matsue Station to Kenchō-mae stop (10 minutes)

Matsue became Lafcadio Hearn's home

MEIMEI-AN TEA-HOUSE
A beautifully restored tea-ceremony site in the castle grounds. Note the two entrances, one low for ordinary folk and a tall entrance for those of high rank.
Open: 09.00–17.00 hrs

Accommodation in Tamatsukuri Onsen
Chorakuen, (tel: (0852) 62-0111). A modern ryokan.
Konya Bekkan (tel: (0852) 62-0331). A farmhouse-style ryokan.
Address for both: Tamayucho, Yatsuka-gun

TSUWANO
A tiny, well-preserved, traditional Japanese castle town set in a high mountain valley. There are good mountain walks in the area, well-maintained temples and shrines, impressive castle ruins on a site above Tsuwano and a variety of designated cycle routes. Tsuwano is nicknamed 'Little Kyōto'. The local tourist information office by the railway station provides walking and cycling maps and details of *minshuku* (inns) and other accommodation and cycle-hire establishments.

Accommodation
Minshuku Wakasugi-no-Yado (tel: (0856) 72-1146).
Ryokan Meigetsu (tel: (0856) 72-0685).
Address for both: Tsuwano-cho, Kanoashi-gun, Shimane-Ken.

HAGI
Hagi is a castle town, port and producer of the distintive pastel-coloured *Hagi-yaki* pottery. It is surrounded by hills on three sides and the Japan Sea to the north.

◆◆◆ CASTLE AND SAMURAI QUARTER
central Hagi
Within the actual castle grounds there is nothing specific to see, but nearby are several

worthwhile places to visit, listed
below:

Horiuchi
Horiuchi district was the
residential area of high-ranking
samurai. It has been well
preserved and many original
houses remain standing behind
distinctive, white-washed stone
garden walls.

Kikuya House
The residence of a wealthy
merchant built in 1604. Preserved
in its original state with furniture
and fittings of the day. Gives one
a feeling of the elegant lifestyle of
well-to-do families of the Edo
period.
Open: 09.00–17.00 hrs

Kumaya Bijutsukan
This is an art museum displaying
works collected by the Kumaya
family who acted as personal
merchants to the Mori clan lords.
The museum is housed in three

Tokoji Temple in Hagi

original warehouses in the
grounds of the family home.
Open: December to February
09.00–17.00 hrs; March to
November 08.30–17.30 hrs

TERAMACHI DISTRICT
A quiet area of temples and
shrines to the southeast of the
castle grounds. Perfect for a
leisurely stroll away from the
crowds.

TOKOJI TEMPLE
eastern Hagi
A Zen temple originally founded
and supported by the Mori
family. Several members of the
clan are buried in tombs behind
the main temples. The path that
leads to them is lined with
hundreds of moss-covered stone
lanterns dedicated to the lords by
their followers.
Open: 08.30–17.00 hrs

KYŪSHŪ AND OKINAWA

Kyūshū is the southernmost and third-largest of Japan's four main islands. Because of its geographical position it became a staging post for the transmission to Japan of Korean and Chinese cultural ideas, the influences of which significantly shaped the development of early Japanese civilisation. The first European explorers, traders and missionaries also arrived via this island, and its people are traditionally less xenophobic, more open and easier to know than their northern cousins. Kyūshū is mountainous and volcanic. The mountain ranges contain many peaks over 5,000 feet (1,525m) and the caldera in Aso-Kuju National Park with the active volcano, Mount Nakadake, at its centre is the largest in the world. There are numerous hot-spring resorts scattered around the island, and the spas of Kyūshū are popular with Japanese tourists. Offshore there are many small islands and south of Kyūshū is the start of the Ryūkyū chain of islands that stretches south almost to Taiwan in the East China Sea. The climate is subtropical and winters are short and dry. Spring and autumn are warm and sunny, and summer is very hot and humid.

How to Get There

The Shinkansen Line terminates at Hakata (Fukuoka) Station. Journey times from Tōkyō and Osaka are 5¾–7¼ hours and 3–4½ hours respectively. By air, travel times are reduced to 1 hour 40 minutes and 1 hour 5 minutes respectively. Costs of train and air travel are comparable, but if you have the time the train journey is interesting in its own right. There is a tourist information office in Hakata Station; English spoken (tel: (092) 431-3003), *open*: 09.00–17.00 hrs.

FUKUOKA

The east of Fukuoka city was originally called Hakata, hence the confusion that sometimes arises in train timetables and maps. Fukuoka, a modern commercial city, is the gateway to Kyūshū and a good base from which to explore the island. The rewards of the economic success of Japan have been put to good use in this city. Stylish, modern architectural developments and a state-of-the-art subway system have been happily married to older dockland, residential and parkland areas. There is thriving night and street life. Fukuoka is well known for its tented food carts that illuminate and line the pavements at night. Under canvas customers squash onto a bench seat in front of a low counter while behind it the cook prepares local specialities and serves beer and sake (hot in the colder, winter months).

There are two subway lines in Fukuoka. Number 1 line links Hakata Station to Tenjin, a major dining, shopping and nightlife area; to Nakasu-Kawabata, another nightlife region (Skunko-bashi at the south end is the best known street for outdoor eating carts); and to Ohori-Koen, an attractive city park surrounding Fukuoka Castle.

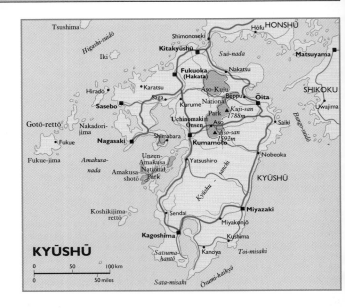

KYŪSHŪ

WHAT TO SEE

◆
SHOFUKU-JI TEMPLE
Gion District
This is the oldest Zen temple in
Japan. It was founded in 1195 by
the priest Eisai who went on to
establish many other important
Rinzai sect Zen temples in Kyōto
and Kamakura. Nowadays it is
rather neglected and feels out of
place in its city-centre location.
Open: 08.30–16.30 hrs
Subway station: Gion

◆
FUKUOKA CASTLE, MAIZURU PARK
AND OHORI PARK
Only a few gates and a simple
turret remain, but the **castle** is
sited on a high hill in **Maizuru
Park** and commands a view of
Fukuoka in every direction. **Ohori
Park** was originally part of the
castle outer defences and some of
it is constructed on the site of the
old moat. In the centre is a large
pond surrounded by willow and
azalea trees, and there is a
museum containing a collection
of Japanese art and tea-making
utensils (*open:* 09.30–17.30 hrs,
closed Mondays).
Fukuoka provides a good base
for exploring Kyūshū.

Accommodation
ANA Hotel Hakata, 3–3–3,
Hakata-ekimae, Hakata-ku,
Fukuoka (tel: (092) 471-7111).
Near Hakata Station. The best
hotel for comfort and economy.
Hotel New Otani Hakata, 1–1–2,
Watanabe-dori, Chuo-ku,
Fukuoka (tel: (092) 714-1111).
English-speaking staff and a
baby-sitting service.

NAGASAKI

Nagasaki is a lovely harbour town with a cosmopolitan atmosphere. It was the first Japanese port to establish trading contacts with foreign countries, and during the 220 years of Japanese seclusion from the rest of the world one tiny island in Nagasaki Bay was allowed to continue as a trading post. Ironically, given its history of communication with the West, Nagasaki was the second target after Hiroshima for atomic bombing.

Nagasaki is 2 hours 20 minutes by rail from Hakata (Fukuoka) Station on the JR Nagasaki Line. The railway station is conveniently connected to the city centre by streetcar, part of a system that links all the main sights. Most of the shopping, dining, nightspots and cultural activities are located in the south of the city. North of the city is the Reme Park and to the west, Inosayama, a mountain-top park offering splendid views of the city. It is also possible to take rickshaw rides around the city (ask at your hotel or at the tourist information office for details). There is a tourist information office outside Nagasaki Station (tel: (0958) 23-3631).

WHAT TO SEE

Nagasaki is not a city with many specific places of interest, but its history, location, scenery, the old city streets, foreign quarters and warm climate tempered with sea breezes make it a place worth exploring, on foot or by streetcar, just for its own sake.

GLOVER MANSION
Oura Tenshudo District
Built by a Scotsman, Thomas Glover in 1863, the house remains much as it was in his day. It is the oldest Western-style building in Japan. Glover married a local geisha girl and is said to have provided the inspiration for *Madame Butterfly*. There are several other old Western residences in the grounds with Nagasaki and its harbour stretched out below.
Open: December to February 08.30–17.00 hrs; March to November 08.00–18.00 hrs

KOFUKIJI TEMPLE
Teramachi District
A Chinese-influenced Obaku Zen temple. The temple buildings are painted red, which sets them apart from traditional Japanese structures. Lovely, grassy gardens with tropical palms and a beautiful main hall, constructed by Chinese carpenters.
Open: 08.00–17.00 hrs

OLD CHINESE SETTLEMENT (TOJIN YASHIKA ATO)
southeastern Nagasaki
In 1698 the shogunate ordered all Chinese in Nagasaki to live in a walled compound in this quarter of the city. The neighbourhood with its narrow, winding streets and busy market places is evocative of an old Chinatown settlement. Nearby Shinchimachi district is the area of present day Chinatown. It is busy and the place to go for good Chinese food.

Kumamoto's powerful castle

hill near the site of the explosion. A bronze statue stands as a symbol of hope for peace, and there are many other sculptures presented by foreign countries. In the **International Culture Hall** there is a display of records and relics of the attack (*open*: 09.00–17.00 hrs; to 18.00 hrs April to October). The park is not that attractive but to visit it is, for most people, an emotional experience.
Open: all year round
Bus: No 1 or 3 streetcar to the Matsuyama cho stop.

KUMAMOTO

Kumamoto is the third-largest city on Kyūshū, but it is at the heart of the island geographically and administratively and was once the southwestern headquarters of the Tokugawa shogunate. For the tourist it is an alternative to Fukuoka as a touring base. It lies at one end of the scenic Yamanami Highway which splits Kyūshū in two and between the two volcanic areas of Aso-Kuju National Park to the east and the Uenzen-Amakusa National Park to the west. Kumamoto is 1½ hours from Hakata (Fukuoka) on the JR Kagoshima Line. Streetcars are the most convenient transportation within the town.

PEACE PARK (HEIWA-KŌEN)
Matsuyama cho
The bomb that exploded on Nagasaki on 9 August 1945 was three times more powerful than the one dropped on Hiroshima. Fortunately it missed the main city and fell on a village on the outskirts of town. Still, over three-quarters of the population of Nagasaki (150,000 people) died. Peace Park was built on a small

SUIZENJI PARK
Suizenji was constructed in 1632 as part of the villa grounds of the Hosokawa clan. It is designed as a miniature version of the old Tokaido highway, between Kyōto and Edo. The park is remarkable for the way generations of gardeners have created a completely artificial landscape from a natural habitat. Each

pruned tree, hill, patch of water or stone has been designed or chosen to represent a natural feature along the Tokaido.
Open: December to mid-March 08.00–17.00 hrs; mid-March to November 07.00–18.00 hrs
Bus: Streetcar to Suizenji-Kōen

◆◆◆ KUMAMOTO CASTLE ✓

There are two major entrances to the castle. The most impressive is the southwest entrance. This approach climbs to the highest point of the main keep and the stone steps pass between walls of massive square stones. From the top of the castle there is a magnificent view of Kumamoto, and Mount Aso smoking in the distance. The castle, built in 1607 by Kiyomasa Kato, was originally constructed with 47 gates and 49 watchtowers. Much of it was burnt down in 1877 but the reconstruction gives a sense of the strength of the original.
The **Prefectural Art Museum** on the west side of the castle has loan exhibitions, and models of *kosun* burial chambers.
Open: 08.30–16.30 hrs; 8.30–17.30 hrs April to September
Closed: 29–31 December

Accommodation
First-class Hotels
Kumamoto Hotel Castle, 4–2, Joto-machi, Kumamoto (tel: (096) 326-3311).
New Sky Hotel, 2, Higashi-Amidaji-cho, Kumamoto (tel: (096) 354-2111).

Moderate Hotels
Hokke Club Kumamoto, 20–1, Torimachi, Kumamoto (tel: (096) 322-5001).

Kumamoto Tokyu Inn, 7–25, Shin-Shigai, Kumamoto (tel: (096) 322-0109).

OKINAWA

The Ryūkyū archipelago is a group of Japanese islands that stretch south from Kyūshū through the Pacific and East China Sea almost to the tip of Taiwan. Their climate is subtropical, and luxurious plants and fruits thrive all year round. Many of the islands are surrounded by coral reefs and fringed by sandy beaches. Okinawa is the largest and most developed island of the group and the one most popular with mainland Japanese tourists. They go there not only for the sun, blue/ green sea and nightlife, but for Okinawan arts, crafts and customs, all of which are markedly different from their own. Okinawa is also the focal point for a network of inter-island ferries that make even remote and barely inhabited islands accessible. Okinawa was occupied by US forces until 1972, when it was handed back to the Japanese. It is still the site of a number of large US military bases.
Okinawa is warm in any season, but October to April is the time most popular with Japanese tourists. June is rainy, and typhoons sometimes occur in September and early October. Earthquakes are common, but they are very rarely felt other than as a gentle rumbling or slight earth tremor.
The south of Okinawa, particularly around the capital Naha, is heavily developed and

KYŪSHŪ AND OKINAWA

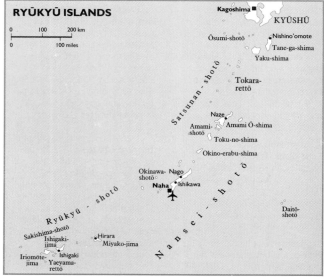

RYŪKYŪ ISLANDS

0 | 100 | 200 km
0 | 100 miles

Kagoshima
KYŪSHŪ
Ōsumi-shotō
Nishino'omote
Tane-ga-shima
Yaku-shima

Satsunan-shotō

Tokara-rettō

Naze
Amami-shotō
Amami Ō-shima
Toku-no-shima

Okino-erabu-shima

Okinawa-shotō
Nago
Naha
Ishikawa

Nansei-shotō

Ryūkyū-shotō

Daitō-shotō

Sakishima-shotō
Ishigaki-jima
Hirara
Miyako-jima
Iriomōte-jima
Ishigaki
Yaeyama-rettō

Coastal beauty at Okinawa

ugly. However, the jumbled mixture of hotels, temples, McDonald's, ice-cream parlours, jogging GIs, Shinto shrines, Japanese tourists, strip joints, karate dojos, old men and women in kimono, and dense traffic fit comfortably together. Much of the north of the island is now also developed, but a few small and traditional fishing and farming villages surrounded by sugar cane and pineapple fields, and unspoilt beaches (nowadays often annexed by the smart hotels) still exist.

Not much remains of the traditional Okinawa culture and to experience this unique Sino-Japanese lifestyle one has to travel to other islands in the Okinawan prefecture. Okinawa is the centre of ferry and air services to these outlying islands.

How To Get There

There are direct flights and sea ferry services to Okinawa (Naha) from Tōkyō, Osaka and Fukuoka. Flight times from mainland Japan are between 1 and 2½ hours, while the ferry takes over 2 days (from Tōkyō) and over 1 day (from Fukuoka). Ferries from Okinawa (Naha) link all the inhabited islands of the Ryūkyū group. An air service links the larger islands.

Flights

Tōkyō (Haneda Airport)—
Okinawa;
Fukuoka—Okinawa.
Contacts:
JAL Tōkyō (tel: (03) 3489-2111)
JAL Okinawa (tel: (0988) 62-3311)
ANA Tōkyō (tel: (03) 5489-8800)
ANA Okinawa (tel: (0988) 66-5111)
JAS Tōkyō (tel: (03) 3432-6111).

Passenger Ferries

Tōkyō (Ariake Pier)—Okinawa;
Fukuoka (Hanata Port)—
Okinawa.
Contacts:
RKK Tōkyō (tel: (03) 3281-1831)
RKK Naha (tel: (0988) 68-1126)
RKK Fukuoka (tel: (092) 291-3362).

Accommodation

First-class Hotel in Naha
Naha Tokyu Hotel, 1002, Ameku, Naha (tel: (098) 868-2151). Has a view of the harbour.

First-class Hotel in North and Central Okinawa
Okinawa Sheraton Hotel, 1478 Kishaba, Kitagusuku-son, Nakajami-gun (tel: (09893) 5-4321). Good views.

CENTRAL AND NORTHERN HONSHŪ AND HOKKAIDŌ

Excluding Tōkyō and Kyōto, which are described in separate sections, this chapter includes the Japan Alps and the historic city of Kanazawa; Tohokū (Northern Honshū), one of the most rural and relatively untouched areas of old Japan; and Hokkaidō, the main northern island of Japan, an area only recently populated and one of long, hard winters and difficult, volcanic terrain.

JAPAN ALPS AND KANAZAWA

The Japan Alps, or the 'roof of Japan' as they are sometimes called, rise in a series of high and jagged, snow-capped peaks in the middle of the Chubu District of Honshū. They cover a vast area and offer a wide variety of hiking, climbing and skiing challenges.

There is a comprehensive network of mountain refuges providing beds, food and provisions, and trekking expeditions through the mountains are more easily planned and more popular.

How To Get There

Matsumoto is 2 hours 20 minutes by JR Chūō Honsen Line from Nagoya and 2 hours 50 minutes in the other direction from Tōkyō (Shinjuku Station). Takayama is 2 hours 55 minutes by JR Takayama Line from Nagoya.

Kamikochi is reached via Matsumoto by the private Matsumoto Dentetsu Line to Shin-Shimajima Station and then a 1 hour 15 minute bus ride.

Matsumoto, an old castle town

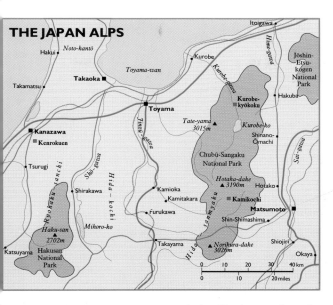

THE JAPAN ALPS

MATSUMOTO

Matsumoto, the main gateway to
the Japan Alps as well as a good
base for exploring central Japan
to the east, is an old castle town
located on a high plateau in a
beautiful alpine setting.

WHAT TO SEE

◆◆◆
MATSUMOTO CASTLE

Also called crow castle (*Karasu-
jo*) because the exterior walls
are mainly black. The five-
tiered donjon built in 1504 is the
oldest in Japan. The castle was
built for serious combat. The
moats are deep and the walls
fitted with many battlements for
firing arrows and guns and
dropping stones. There is a
moon-viewing turret and a
museum of local history. The

castle is a 20 minute walk north
of the station.
Open: 08.30–17.00 hrs.
Closed: 29 December to 3 January

◆◆
JAPAN UKIYOE MUSEUM

A vast collection of woodblock
prints (*ukiyoe*) housed in a
relatively modern, elegant
building.
Open: Tuesday to Sunday
10.00–17.00 hrs.
Closed: Mondays and 29
December to 3 January

◆◆
TATEYAMA—KUROBE
ALPINE ROUTE TOUR

This is a spectacular tour through
the mountains using a variety of
transport. It starts at Shinano-
Omachi (1 hour from Matsumoto
on the JR Oito Line) and ends at
Toyama using buses, cable-cars,

trains and your own feet. The route is open late April to the end of November.

NAGANO

Nagano Prefecture has been selected to host the 1998 Winter Olympic Games. Nagano city will host the opening and closing ceremonies. Access to the city is from Tōkyō's Ueno Station on the JR Shint-su Line (2 hours 50 minutes) or from Matsumoto on the JR Chūō Line (55 minutes).

Accommodation
Matsumoto Tokyu Inn, 1–3–21, Fukashi, Matsumoto (tel: (0263) 36-0109). Facing the station.

KAMIKOCHI

The bus route from Shin-Shimashima to Kamikochi (1 hour 20 minutes), which is over a narrow and twisting mountain road, is open from the end of April to the beginning of November. Kamikochi is a high valley surrounded by the Japan Alps and if offers some of the best hiking trails in Japan. The Azusa River that runs down the valley is wide and sparkling clean. The area is very busy during the summer months and vacant accommodation is scarce. Early spring and mid-autumn (October) are the best times to visit. Mountain huts with comfortable accommodation are found along the hiking trails and camping/hiking equipment may be hired around the bus station. Reserve well in advance for any accommodation.

Accommodation
Kamikochi Imperial Hotel, Azumimura, Kamikochi (tel: (0263) 95-2001).

TAKAYAMA

Takayama is situated in the mountainous Hida district of West Central Japan. The city has been modernised but there remain many temples and traditional buildings. Takayama holds two nationally famous festivals each year. The spring festival of the Hie Shrine (14 and 15 April) and the autumn festival of the Hachiman Shrine (9 and 10 October). Accommodation around these times needs to be booked months ahead.

WHAT TO SEE

HIDA MINZOKU-MURA (HIDA FOLK VILLAGE)
The village is an open-air exhibition of more than 30 relocated, traditional Hida farmhouses and buildings, some now house folkcraft workshops displaying domestic artefacts. Situated a short bus journey from Takayama bus station.
Open: 08.30–17.00 hrs

MORNING MARKETS
A daily market (07.00 hrs to noon) held in front of Takayama Jinya Manor House and along one bank of the Miyagawa River. Local farmers bring their produce for sale.

SANNO-MACHI
Ten minutes walk from the station is the old merchant district with houses, tea-shops and inns dating from the mid-Edo period. Shops in the area sell local products such as lacquerware, pottery and sake.

Morning market at Takayama

SHORENJI TEMPLE

A Zen temple transported in 1960 from the Shokawa Valley, part of which was flooded to make a reservoir. The size of the Main Hall built in 1504 is particularly impressive. *Shojin-ryori* (Zen vegetarian food) is served at the temple and it is worth stopping here for lunch.
Open: November to March 08.30–17.00 hrs; April to October 08.00–18.00 hrs

TAKAYAMA JINYA

Eight minutes walk from the station are the white-washed old provincial government offices. They have been well preserved and you may visit the audience chambers, the interrogation rooms and the areas previously reserved for high officials. There are gardens at the back and the rice store-rooms where the shogunate's rice tax was collected.
Open: 08.45–16.30 hrs

Accommodation

Hotel
Takayama Green Hotel, 2–180, Nishino-isshikicho, Takayama (tel: (0577) 33-5500).

Ryokans
Hishuya, 1–464, Kamiokamoto-machi, Takayama (tel: (0577) 33-4001). A genuine, quiet Japanese inn.
Sogo Palace Takayama, 54, Suehirocho, Takayama (tel: (0577) 33-5000). A modern, international hotel.

KANAZAWA

One of the beguiling characteristics of the Japanese is their faith in the unity of heaven and earth. Kanazawa is a city where this unselfconscious union of spiritual and worldly affairs can be experienced to the full. It is in part an old Japanese castle town with a thriving reputation as a centre of traditional religion, arts and crafts, especially Noh theatre. At the same time, it is a very modern city with sophisticated shops and nightlife.

How to Get There

Kanazawa is 2½ hours from Kyōto by train on the JR Hokuriku Line and 1 hour from Tōkyō by plane (via Komatsu Airport) on JAL, ANA and JAS flights from Haneda Airport. A visit to Kanazawa may also be included in a crossing of the Japan Alps by train from Tōkyō. Total journey time is about 6 hours with changes of train at Matsumoto, Takayama and Toyama.

WHAT TO SEE

◆◆◆

KENROKUEN GARDEN ✓

One of the easiest places to find and a useful reference point for later exploration, is Kenrokuen Garden, Kanazawa's most famous attraction. Kenrokuen, once the private garden of the Maeda lords who ruled the city for three generations, is officially categorized as one of Japan's three best gardens (the Japanese love to classify, whether it is Views, Shrines or Living Artists). Situated beneath the castle mound, now marked only by its original entrance gate, Kenrokuen combines perfectly the six qualities by which a park is judged: size, seclusion, running water, views, artificiality and age. *Open*: 1 March to 15 October 07.00–18.00 hrs; 16 October to 28 February 08.00–16.30 hrs

Tranquil Kenrokuen Garden is judged to be one of the best in Japan

◆◆◆
NAGAMACHI SAMURAI QUARTER

The old samurai quarter is in the Nagamachi district which starts just behind the 109 Korinbo department store. Many of the samurai houses are reproductions, but still worth seeing for their austere charm. The **Nomura Family House**, once the home of a well-to-do samurai warrior, has been maintained in its original condition and it is open for visiting. The design of the interior is severe but elegant with a rich use of cypress, ebony and persimmon woods.
Open: 08.30–16.30 hrs; 8.30–17.30 hrs April to September
Closed: 29–31 December.

◆◆
HIGASHIYAMA AND EASTERN PLEASURE QUARTER

The Utatsyma Mountain rises behind the east bank of the Asano River in the Higashiyama District and overlooks the city. Its sides are peppered with 40 individual Buddhist and Shinto temples, some still in use, others in varying degrees of moss-covered decay. On the flat summit is a delightful 'natural' park with waymarked paths through a landscape of many different trees and shrubs. The **Eastern Pleasure Quarter** in the Higashiyama district was set aside in 1820 as an entertainment area for high ranking citizens. The most talented and beautiful of 'free' geisha girls provided evenings of music, dancing, conversation and perhaps other more intimate pleasures. The Eastern area is distinguished by a neat row of geisha tea-houses.

Oyama Shrine, in Kanazawa

Some of the old atmosphere can still be experienced along Higashi main street. **Shima-ke**, the fifth house down the street on the left going east, is an elegant former geisha house open for viewing.
Open: 09.00–17.00 hrs
Closed: Monday

Accommodation

First-class Hotels
Holiday Inn Kanazawa, 1–10, Horikawacho, Kanazawa (tel: (0762) 23-1111). English-speaking staff.
Kanazawa Tokyu Hotel, 2–1–1, Korinbo, Kanazawa (tel: (0762) 31-2411).

Ryokans
Hakuunro Hotel, He-25, Yuwakucho, Kanazawa (tel: (0762) 35-1111). Forty minutes by bus from Kanazawa. Scenic location.
Miyabo, 3, Shimokakinokibatake, Kanazawa (tel: (0762) 31-4228). Traditional atmosphere. The rooms open onto beautiful gardens.

CENTRAL AND NORTHERN HONSHŪ

TOHOKŪ (NORTHERN HONSHŪ)

Tohokū, the northernmost region of Honshū, has severe winters and a mountainous terrain. This together with the area's distance from Tōkyō, long farming tradition and history of local crafts has restricted serious commercial development, and Tohokū remains one of the regions of Japan least affected by industrialisation. It has a rural, untouched attractiveness, marred only by some of the tourist facilities in the most popular areas of the national parks and historic towns. Outside these places tourists are not particularly catered for. Travel to Tohokū is quite easy via the Tohokū Shinkansen or the Yamagata Shinkansen, but once there and off the beaten track local train journey times are slower and routes are more complicated. Tohokū has very cold, snowy winters and dry mild summers. The main tourist season is in the summer. The first 10 days of August are particularly busy with big festivals in Sendai, Akita and Aomori. Spring begins early from mid-April. The cherry blossom viewing season is late April. Autumn begins in September and the trees take on their rich full colours by early October. The region is divided into northern, central and southern.

NORTHERN TOHOKŪ

◆◆◆
HIROSAKI

Hirosaki was Tohokū's cultural and political centre until the beginning of the Meiji period when Aomori, now a modern and busy port town, usurped its place. Unlike Aomori, Hirosaki escaped war-time bombing, but it has nevertheless still lost much of its architectural heritage. Fortunately, despite a plethora of modern buildings, the city retains some of its old winding alleys and has an appealing attractiveness enhanced by the friendliness of the town's people, the thriving local craft traditions and some well-maintained sites of cultural interest. Hirosaki is easily and best explored on foot. The tourist information office by the station provides a map and information in English.

Hirosaki is connected to Morioka by a direct rail line. Travelling time is about 4 hours and there are several departures daily.

Accommodation
Ishiba Ryokan, 55, Moto Teramachi, Hirosaki (tel: (0172) 32-9118). Modern ryokan with an old-fashioned atmosphere.

◆◆◆
MORIOKA

Morioka is a castle town founded by the feudal lord Nambu in the 16th century, and is also an old-established provincial university town. It is a charming place of much character with many temples, an old merchant quarter, a vigorous cultural life and a successful craft industry. Morioka is 2½–3½ hours by Tohokū Shinkansen from Ueno Station in Tōkyō.

Accommodation
Morioka Terminal Hotel, 1–44, Morioka-Ekimaedori, Morioka (tel: (0196) 25-1211).
Hotel Royal Morioka, 1–11–11, Saien, Morioka (tel: (0196) 53-1331).

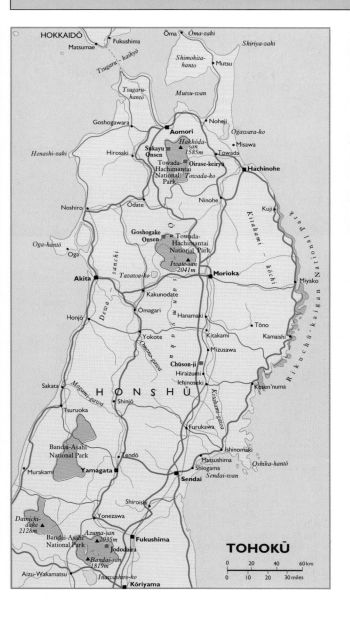

TOHOKU

A lake in a crater: Towada-ko

◆◆◆
TOWADA-HACHIMANTAI NATIONAL PARK

The park which is northwest of Morioka, includes Towada-ko (Lake Towada)—the surrounding area of which is of exceptional scenic beauty—and the volcanic district, Hachimantai Plateau. The lake is formed in a giant crater 23 square miles (58.5 hectares) in area and over 1,000 feet (305 m) deep. Around it the gentle mountain ranges provide good hiking and skiing. There are many *onsen* (hot springs) in the area. Sukayu Onsen to the north, which has a 1,000 person bath, is one of the better known. The pretty Oirase-keiryū (Oirase Valley) district to the northeast is also popular with walkers, particularly in the autumn when the valley is especially beautiful. There is a frequent bus service from mid-April to early November directly from Morioka and Aomori to Lake Towada.

Hachimantai is a mountainous area of volcanic activity better known for its numerous onsen and thermal resorts than scenic beauty. Goshogake Onsen and Toshichi Onsen are two such hot-spring centres, where people go to soothe away city stress and other more serious ailments. Mixed bathing is still the norm.

◆◆◆
RIKUCHU-KAIGAN NATIONAL PARK

This stretch of rugged rocky coastline is famous for its high cliffs, fantastic rock formations, small fishing villages and marine life. It was until very recently an inaccessible area, but nowadays with the building of two private railways it is easier to explore. Buses go from Morioka to Kuji (3 hours 10 minutes) and from here you can take a train on the Kita Rias Line to Shimanokoshi on the coast. From here you can bus up and down the coastal zone of the park.

CENTRAL AND SOUTHERN TOHOKŪ

SENDAI

Sendai is the largest city in Tohokū. It was flattened in World War II and has since been rebuilt along the lines of any modern Japanese city. It is not unattractive but there is nothing exceptional there. It is, however, a reasonably good base from which to explore the neighbouring Yamagata Prefecture, a rural district where life is very much in traditional Tohokū style. Sendai is 2 hours by Tohokū Shinkansen from Tōkyō's Ueno Station.

MATSUSHIMA

Matsushima-Kaigan is 40 minutes by Senseki Line from Sendai. This is the main stopping point for the famed Matsushima Bay, which is dotted with countless pine-covered small islands which may be visited by pleasure boat. Some are inhabited while others are just tiny islets. The bay is regarded as one of Japan's 'Three Famous Views' (the other two are Amano-hashidate, north of Kyōto and Miyajima, near Hiroshima).

HIRAIZUMI

During the 11th and 12th centuries the northern branch of the Fujiwara clan turned Hiraizumi into a town that at the time rivalled Kyōto. They built many temples and palaces from the proceeds of the gold they mined in the area although today very few remain standing. The most famous of those that do is The Golden Hall of Chuson-ji Temple (recently fully restored). It is a marvel of lacquer and gold leaf decoration. The farmland areas around Hiraizumi are worth visiting for their large and fine farmhouses. Hiraizumi itself is a small historic country town. Hiraizumi is 10 minutes by train from Ichinoseki, which is on the Tohokū Line. There are also bus services between Ichinoseki and Hiraizumi.

Accommodation

Matsushima Kanko Hotel, 115, Chonai, Matsushima (tel: (0223) 54-2121).
Sendai Hotel, 1–10–25, Chuo, Sendai (tel: (022) 225-5171).
Shirayama Ryokan, 115–6, Shirasan, Hiraizumi-cho (tel: (0191) 46-2883).

BANDAI-ASAHI NATIONAL PARK

The national park occupies an area to the west and south of Fukushima and to the north of Aizu-Wakamatsu. It includes some of the most pretty, interesting and accessible mountain and lake scenery in Japan. Azuma-san (the Azuma Mountains) near Fukushima are ideal for moderate hiking tours. Access to Azuma-san is from Jododaira bus station on the Bandai-Azuma Sky Line road. Fukushima is 1½ hours on the Tohokū Shinkansen Line from Ueno Station in Tōkyō. Bandai-Kogen, at the centre of Bandai Plateau, is 40 minutes from Fukushima on the Sky Line road or 3 hours on the scenic Bandai-Azuma Lake Line road (both closed early November to late April).

HOKKAIDŌ

Until the beginning of this
century Hokkaidō, a wild and
inhospitable place, was not
considered a inhabitable area
by the Japanese. They visited
and settled only the island's
coastal regions to fish and
collect seaweed. Some Ainu,
Japan's original indigenous
people, lived in the interior, but
there were no inland Japanese
settlements or agriculture.
Shortage of space on the other
main islands, coupled with the
return after 1945 of many
Japanese colonists from abroad,
led to the first real development
of the island and today over 5
million people live there. It is
still, however, the least populous
region of Japan. There are few
cultural or historical reasons to
visit Hokkaidō, but for those who
enjoy the outdoors it offers
mountains and wide open
landscapes, and the opportunity
to ski, hike and bicycle.
Hokkaidō is expensive to get to
and once there, because of its
size and sparseness of public
transport, it is difficult and costly
to explore.
Sapporo, capital of Hokkaidō;
Hakodate, the earliest settled port
town; and Daisetsuzan National
Park; these are three places
definitely worth visiting.
Hokkaidō has long, cold winters
that stretch from November to
April, and short spring, summer
and autumn seasons. Mid-
summer is warm and dry and a
time of many blooming flowers.

How to Get There
Train—The Hokutosei limited
express sleeper train travels
between Tōkyō (Ueno Station)
and Sapporo. Three departures a
day, about a 15-hour journey.
Air—JAL, ANA and JAS flights are
scheduled to Sapporo from
Tōkyō and Osaka. There are also
services from many other cities.
Ferry—There are ferry services
from Tōkyō to Tomakomai or
Kushiro and from many towns on
the coast of Tohokū, eg Oma-
Hakodate, Aomori-Muroran and
Noheji-Hakodate.
Once There
There is a rail and bus network
on Hokkaidō and internal flights
between major cities.

SAPPORO
Sapporo is a large modern city
laid out on a grid system. There
are many parks, but it is not a
place to visit for tourist attractions,
more a base from which to plan
and explore the wilderness areas
of Hokkaidō. The city does,
however, have an active and
famous nightlife and the Susukino
district is as exciting and risqué
as anything in Tōkyō. The tourist
information office is at Sapporo
Station.

WHAT TO SEE

NATURAL HISTORY MUSEUM
OF AGRICULTURE
In the grounds of the University's
Botanical Gardens, housed in the
former home of John Batchelor,
an Englishman who was keenly
interested in the Ainu culture and
people. There is a good
collection of Ainu artefacts.
Open: 29 April to 3 November,
Tuesday to Sunday 09.00–16.00
hrs
Closed: Mondays and 4
November to 28 April

Accommodation

Sapporo Grand Hotel, 4–2, Nishi, Kita-1, Chuo-ku, Sapporo (tel: (011) 261-3311). Old-established, Western-style hotel.

HAKODATE

In 1854 when Japan abandoned the isolationist policy of the previous two centuries, Hakodate became one of the country's first treaty ports. Foreign traders, especially Russians, settled in the port and formed a community in the Motomachi Area where a number of old Western-style buildings still remain. Hakodate

Hokkaidō, on Japan's northern tip, was a wild and uninhabited place until its development from the beginning of this century

was the original capital of Hokkaidō and it remains its historical centre. Hakodate is 3 hours 50 minutes by rail from Sapporo and 1¼ hours by air from Tōkyō.

WHAT TO SEE

GORYOKAKU FORTRESS

A Western-style fort built in 1864 by the Tokugawa shogunate to protect northern Japan from the Russians. Instead, the fort was occupied by samurai who supported the deposed shogunate against the Imperial Army of the Meiji government. Now a park area and open to the public. *Open*: late April to late October 08.00–19.45 hrs; late October to late April 09.00–17.45 hrs

MOTOMACHI AREA

The old foreign community settled in this area, and some of their houses remain as well as a Russian Orthodox Church with onion domes.

MOUNT HAKODATE

The day and, especially, night views of the city and harbour from the top of Mount Hakodate are very beautiful. There is a cable-car to the top from Jujigai which operates 10.00–20.50 hrs (21.50 hrs, 26 April to 31 October) and takes 5 minutes. It is also possible to hike to the top (trail open late April to late October).

Accommodation

Standard Hotel
Hakodate Kokusai Hotel, 5–10, Otemachi, Hakodate (tel: (0138) 23-5151).

Economy Hotels
Hotel Hakodate Royal, 16–19, Omoricho, Hakodate (tel: (0138) 26-8181).
Hotel Hakodateyana, 19–1, Motomachi, Hakodate (tel: (0138) 23-7237).

DAISETSUZAN NATIONAL PARK

The largest national park in Japan and one of the most unspoiled. A network of hiking paths gives access to most areas of the park and to many of the mountain tops, none of which rise much above 7,000 feet (2,133 m). Most of the accommodation available in the park includes access to hot-spring baths.

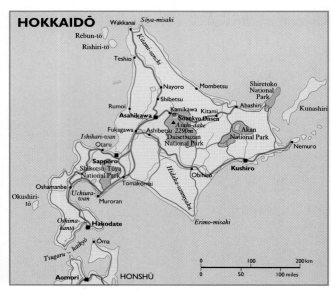

PEACE AND QUIET
Countryside and Wildlife in Japan

by Paul Sterry

The Japan archipelago is a fascinating destination for anyone with an interest in scenery and wildlife. The long string of islands runs along the east coast of Asia from South Korea northwards to Russia. As a consequence of the wide latitude embraced, an extraordinary range of climate and vegetation can be found along the length of the country, from sub-tropical forests in the south to a winter landscape of snow and frozen sea ice in the north of Hokkaidō.

Much of Japan is mountainous, culminating in Fuji-san at 12,388 feet (3,776m). The slopes of many of the mountains are cloaked in forest, but although they may look natural, man's influence has been strongly felt here and most of the woodland has been degraded or replanted. But nowhere is man's influence more pronounced than on the lowland plains: here agriculture dominates, with a neat rural landscape of farms and rice paddies. It all contrasts sharply with the hustle and bustle of cities like Tōkyō.

Contrasts are a recurring theme throughout Japan and this is perhaps most strikingly evident in the attitude towards wildlife and the environment. Birds, mammals and flowers are depicted and revered throughout art and literature, and yet this reverence appears not to conflict in Japanese culture with a pragmatic and seemingly unsympathetic view of the environment as a resource to be exploited. This attitude has led not only to the wholesale destruction of Japanese landscapes and environments (which inspired the art) but also to exploitation of the natural world far beyond the boundaries of the country.

For example, Japan is one of the major consumers of tropical hardwoods from the rainforests of southeast Asia. It is also a driving force behind moves to keep commercial whaling a looming future threat just when whale populations are beginning to show signs of recovering from the slaughter of the last five decades. As a result of these contrasting attitudes, many visitors to Japan who are sympathetic towards environmental issues leave with mixed feelings about the Japanese way of life and the global benefits, or otherwise, of its economic miracle.

In and Around Tōkyō

Considering the number of people who live and work in Tōkyō and the amount of building and development that has been undertaken in recent years, it is a wonder that there is any wildlife interest left in the city at all. Yet although many of the parks and gardens in Tōkyō and the surrounding towns are manicured and landscaped to a point where they have ceased to be attractive to wildlife, there are several areas still worth exploring.

The Meiji Jingū (Shrine) is on most visitors' itineraries, and in addition to the shrine itself, the surrounding land has beautiful woodlands and lakes; the entrance is near Meiju-jingū Station on the Chiyoda Line or Harajuku Station on the Yamanote Line. Look for azure-winged magpies in the woodland here – these birds are perennial favourites of Japanese artists. The ponds and lakes attract a wide variety of waterbirds, including elegant Mandarin ducks.

The male mandarins are unmistakable, with orange, chestnut and white on the head, a red bill and orange, fan-shaped inner wing feathers. Females are more sombre but have a conspicuous white spectacle and eye-stripe.

Ueno Park, near Ueno Station on the Yamanote Line, contains the Ueno Zoo, the Water Zoo and the Lotus Pond, the latter attracting waterbirds including Mandarin ducks and cormorants.

Oi Wild Bird Park near Ryutsu-senta Station is another good spot for waterbirds. It also attracts migrant waders during spring and autumn.

Pools, reedbeds and mudflats can all be found at Gyotoku, close to the shores of Tōkyō Bay. The reserve here can be viewed from a bird observatory near Gyotoku School, which is a short walk south from either Minami-Gyotoku Station or Gyotoku Station, both on the Tozai Line. Herons, egrets, terns and wildfowl can be seen, and if you are very lucky a Baikal teal. Forest birds and giant flying squirrels can be found on the wooded slopes and in the bamboo around Yakuo-in Temple, and it's worth exploring the area from Takao-san-guchi Station on the Keio Line.

The Imperial Palace Moat, in central Tōkyō, can easily be reached from Tōkyō Station and makes an excellent destination for anyone seeking the natural world in the heart of the city.

Nikkō National Park

Nikkō National Park contains some of the most attractive landscapes on Honshū, with lakes, rivers and wooded mountains. It is easily reached by road or rail from Tōkyō, Nikkō being about two hours from Tōkyō by rail. Within the town can be found the Botanical Gardens and Nikkō Museum, where there are displays about the national park.

Lake Chuzenji is a central feature of the park. At its eastern end are the dramatic Kegon Falls, 328 feet (100m) high. Birds to look out for include brown dippers, wildfowl and grebes. Japanese macaques are sometimes seen from the road between Nikkō and the lake, and sika deer live in the surrounding forests.

A nature trail runs along the northern shores of Lake Chuzenji and to the north there are several trails across the marshy Senjogabara plateau, where marsh plants, ducks and waders can be found. Paths also lead up towards the mountains of Taro-san and Sannoboshizan, passing through forested areas, which are good for birds.

Jōshin-etsu Kōgen National Park

Within this large area, the forested resort of Karuizawa makes an ideal base for exploration. The town lies to the northwest of Tōkyō and is most

easily reached from Ueno Station
in Tōkyō on the Shin-etsu Line to
Karuizawa Station (a 2 hour
journey). In addition to
woodlands of white birch and
Japanese larch on the mountain
slopes, there are hot springs.
There is a Wild Bird Wood close
to Hoshino Spa and the Nishiku-
Iriguchi bus stop, where there is
a nature trail and bird feeders.
Numerous trails lead from
Karuizawa into the hills.

Chubū-Sangaku (Japan Alps) National Park

Kamikochi lies at the heart of the
Japan Alps, in one of the most
beautiful settings in the whole of
Japan. It can be reached by car
on Route 158 west from
Matsumoto and then north at
Nakanoyum Onsen or by rail
from Matsumoto to Shin-
shimashima, then by bus.
From the main car park in
Kamikochi, a trail runs along the
south side of the Azusa River. To
the east is a dramatic suspension
bridge and to the west is the
Tashiro-ike pond. There are also
several other trails that lead into
the high mountains.

Chichibu-Tama National Park

This large national park lies
northwest of Tōkyō between Kofu
and Chichibu; the main areas of
access are from the separate
valleys in which Chichibu and
Okutama lie. Rail links exist
between both towns and Tōkyō.
The park boasts lakes, dramatic
gorges and wooded slopes and
several trails allow exploration of
the area. A cable car
approaches the summit of
Mitake-san and the gorges at

The deep valley of Kamikochi

Mitake and Hatonosu can be
viewed from trails.

Fuji-Hakone-Izu National Park

Fuji-san at 12,388 feet (3,776m)
is the highest peak in Japan and
dominates this spectacular
national park. Although often
shrouded in mist and cloud, the
symmetrical peak, capped with
snow, is a wonderful sight on a
clear day, and the forested
slopes and lakes to the north
make this a superb destination.
The best place from which to
explore the area is the town of
Gotemba, which can be reached
from Tōkyō either by car or by
rail from Tōkyō's Shinjuku

PEACE AND QUIET

*Lake Ashino, Fuji-Hakone-Izu
National Park*

Station on the Gotemba Line.
From Gotemba, buses transport
visitors to Shin Gogome, the Fifth
Station, and from here it is an
eight-hour walk to the summit.

Bandai-Asahi National Park

This national park is situated near
Aizu-Wakamatsu to the northeast
of Tōkyō and buses can be taken
to Goshikinuma Iriguchi or
Yama-no-ie, both close to Hibara
Lake. The area is dominated by
volcanic peaks, and the rivers,
lakes and marshes are home to
waders and wildfowl. There is a
marsh nature trail starting at
Goshikinuma.

Shiretoko Hanto (Peninsula), Hokkaidō

The Shiretoko Peninsula, which
juts out into the Sea of Okhotsk, is
one of the most remote regions
of Japan. The tip of the peninsula

is a national park and can be
reached by road, Route 334
running along the north of the
peninsula and Route 335 along
the south. However, the roads do
not run to the tip of the peninsula
but cross from Utoro in the north
to Rausu in the south.
The tip of the peninsula is
dominated by the volcanic peak
of Io-san and three other
mountains. There are several
hiking trails available in the area
– one starts at Kamuiwakka
waterfall – and visitors should
enquire in Rausu for further
details. In particular, the forested
walk around the Shiretoko Five
Lakes is especially rewarding.
During the summer months,
there is even a chance of seeing
a brown bear, the area being
one of their remaining
strongholds.
The scenery is perhaps at its
most dramatic during the winter
months, with the peaks and
steep, forested valleys covered

in snow and sea ice fringing the shoreline. For the naturalist, it is the Steller's sea-eagles that frequent the shores in the winter that are the most exciting wildlife attraction. Numbers build up during the winter and several thousand may be present as spring approaches.

The best way to see the eagles is to drive along Route 335 north from Rausu before dawn to watch them leaving their roosts in the forests just before it gets properly light. They spend the day on the sea ice and then return to roost in the late afternoon.

Whooper Swans at Odaito, Hokkaidō

Odaito lies on the east coast of Hokkaidō, sheltered from the seas of the Nemuro Straits by the long sand spit of Notsuke. It can be reached by road by driving south from Rausu on the Shiretoko Peninsula or north on Route 244 from Nemuro. Alternatively, catch a bus from Nemuro Shibetsu south to Odaito. The coastal scenery is dramatic and, in winter, whooper swans and Steller's sea-eagles appear and form a wonderful wildlife spectacle. During the summer months, the saltmarsh and mudflats on the landward side of Notsuke sand spit are the haunt of both resident and migrant waders and wildfowl. In autumn, birds such as brent geese, goldeneye and pintail appear, but as winter progresses, much of the area freezes, forcing many of the birds to move away. However, the icy conditions do not deter whooper swans, and several thousand may be present

towards the end of winter. There is a swan observatory on the coastal road south from Odaito where the swans are fed, some of them becoming accustomed to human presence.

Lake Furen, Hokkaidō

Lake Furen is another excellent area for coastal birdwatching. To reach it drive east from Kishuro and view the area from the road near the junction with Route 243. Waders and wildfowl are especially numerous in spring and autumn, and the surrounding forests harbour sika deer and woodland birds.

Rishiri-Rebun-Sarobetsu National Park, Hokkaidō

This is the most northerly of Hokkaidō's national parks and is accessible from Wakkanai. This settlement is at least an eight-hour drive north from Sapporo and visitors may wish to consider flying. The main features of the national park are the islands of Rishiri, with the volcanic Mount Rishiri at its heart, and Rebun and the Sarobetsu Natural Flower Garden, best visited for its natural display of alpine flowers during May and June.

Marshland birds breed in abundance in the national park and the area is a staging post for migrant ducks and swans heading south in the autumn. Woodland birds abound in the forests, and brown bears, deer and squirrels may appear.

Akan National Park, Hokkaidō

Akan National Park is a wonderful area both for scenic beauty and for wildlife. It is dominated by volcanic peaks, but lakes and vast forests add variety. Akan lies in the east of Hokkaidō and can be reached from Kushiro to the south either by road on Route 240 or by rail to Kawayu Station, which is to the east of Lake Kussharo. Kussharo is the largest volcanic lake in Japan and a focal point of the national park. A few ducks and grebes can be found in summer and autumn, but in winter most of the lake freezes over. At the southern end, hot springs at Wakoto Hanto (Peninsula) keep some of the bays open and whooper swans might be seen.

Daisetsuzan National Park, Hokkaidō

Daisetsuzan National Park lies in the centre of Hokkaidō and is one of the most scenic parts of the island, dominated as it is by a series of volcanic parks. It is Japan's largest national park and its attractions include large tracts of forest, rivers, gorges and ice fields. The entrance to the park from the north is on Route 39, 9 miles (15km) east of Kamikawa.

Shikotsu-Tōya National Park, Hokkaidō

This large national park lies in southwest Hokkaidō, not far from Sapporo. Among its scenic attractions are volcanoes, caldera lakes, hot springs and forests; lakes Toya and Shikotsu, the latter the deepest lake in Japan, give the park its name. Lake Shikotsu can easily be reached by driving south from Sapporo by car or by bus to Shikotsu-kohan. A road runs around the shoreline and there

are numerous trails, including a nature trail which starts from the car park to the east of the lake.

Japanese Cranes at Kushiro, Hokkaidō

Kushiro is a town on the southeast coast of Hokkaidō, connected by road and rail to Sapporo and with a regular ferry service to Tōkyō. Although lacking any intrinsic wildlife interest, it is, however, an excellent base from which to witness one of the most outstanding wildlife spectacles on Japan. During the winter months, when most other birds have departed south to escape the cold weather, several hundred Japanese cranes visit the marshes, rivers and fields to the north of the town.

One of the best places to see the cranes feeding is at the Tancho no-Sato observatory, which is reached by driving west from Kushiro on Route 38 and then north on Route 240 – the road to Akan National Park. The observatory is clearly marked after about 15 miles (25km) and is open from 08.30 hrs. The best months are January and February, when the cranes are feeding in the stubble fields, their diet supplemented each day with grain. Towards the end of the season the cranes often begin displaying to each other and the sight of pairs of these beautiful birds engaged in ritual dances is a memorable one. Japanese cranes can also be seen in smaller numbers at the Ito Sanctuary, which can be reached by driving north on Route 284 from Kushiro. Alternatively, they can be seen

An elegant Japanese crane

roosting in the shallow waters of the Setsurigawa. At this site they must be viewed from the bridge over the river, which is reached by forking right off Route 284 at Watanabe Kyuji-ba. It is essential to be there at dawn for the best views of the birds.

Formerly widspread in Japan, the Japanese crane was thought to be extinct at the turn of the century. A remnant population on Hokkaidō survived, however, and has been allowed to flourish thanks to the establishment of sanctuaries. Several hundred now survive on this island and comprise about a third of the entire world population. These large birds stand over 59 inches (150cm) high, and have distinctive, mostly white plumage, black plumes, a black neck and white nape with a red crown. The birds breed in vast marshland areas in southeast Hokkaidō. Pairs stay together for life. Cranes feature strongly in Japanese art and mythology, being revered not only for their elegant appearance and grace, but also for their fidelity.

Aso-Kuju National Park, Kyūshū

This park in northern central Kyūshū is dominated by Mount Aso, an active volcano which lies in the largest volcanic crater in the world. To visit Mount Aso you can either catch a bus from Aso Station or drive either from Aso Station or Okamizu Station to the west. Because the volcano is active and potentially dangerous, there may be occasions when it is not possible to reach the rim of the crater. Look for white-rumped swifts around Mount Aso: they nest on the walls of the crater and can be recognised by their scythe-shaped wings, black plumage with conspicuous white rump and markedly forked tail.

Arasaki Crane Reserve, Kyūshū

Arasaki in southwestern Kyūshū is by far the best place in Japan to see large numbers of cranes. Surrounding the small town are rice fields and it is these that attract the cranes in the winter months. Arasaki lies between Kumamoto and Kagoshima, just to the north of Route 3.

The best months to see the cranes, which migrate here from Asia, are between November and February. Several thousand hooded cranes are usually present and are joined by up to a thousand white-naped cranes. However, a few individuals of other crane species occasionally join these flocks. There is a car park and bird observatory to the north of Arasaki village, the birds fed daily by the warden.

Most cranes are migratory; hooded and white-naped cranes are no exception. Neither species breeds in Japan, both nesting in Russia and migrating south to spend the winter months on Kyūshū in Japan and on the Chinese mainland. Hooded cranes have mainly black plumage with a white neck and head and black and red on the forehead. White-naped cranes are extremely elegant birds. The plumage is mainly grey but the neck and head are white, and a red patch around the eye is surrounded by a black border. At their wintering grounds at Arasaki, they are occasionally joined by demoiselle cranes, common cranes and even Siberian white cranes in some winters.

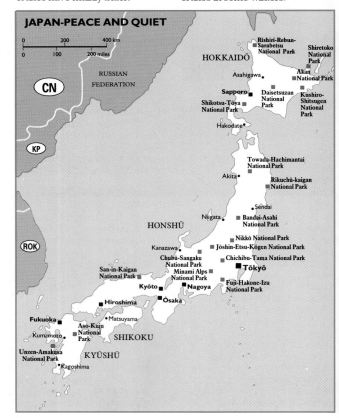

JAPAN-PEACE AND QUIET

FOOD AND DRINK

It is said that Chinese food is for the pleasure of the stomach, French food for the pleasure of the nose, and Japanese food for the pleasure of the eye. This is only partly true of Japanese food, which to be really enjoyed should be tasted with the tongue, the heart and the eye. Traditional formal meals are cooked and presented by the Japanese chef with the intention of inspiring both the senses and the spirit of the recipients of the food. Season, location, religious and/or cultural factors are considered before the menu is planned. The food being served and the manner of its presentation then dictate the nature of the serving bowls or plates to be used. Ceramic, wood or lacquer tableware is selected for each dish according to which harmonises most

Noodles are a Japanese favourite

aesthetically with the colour, texture and appearance of the food. In the centre of the chosen plate or bowl the food is arranged, almost sculpted, and delicately garnished before being served. The meal reflects philosophical as well as culinary attitudes.

Of course, the chance of being a guest at a traditional meal is rare even for the Japanese, but there is much Japanese food to enjoy beneath these lofty heights. Apart from an early Chinese influence, Japanese cuisine has developed in a state of isolation. Its style is unique. Buddhist beliefs, which forbade the eating of flesh foods, also influenced the Japanese diet and the main ingredients were rice, vegetables, pickles, seafood, soya-bean products and fruit. It is ironic that nowadays, when this type of diet is highly recommended by nutritionists, the Japanese are eating more meat, dairy products and what

FOOD AND DRINK

must be the worst, most lifeless white bread in the world. The McDonald's burger bar in Tōkyō is reputed to have the highest turnover in the whole chain. At a Japanese meal individual dishes are served in small amounts but in greater variety than in the West. They are all served at the same time rather than in courses, and the order in which they are eaten is a matter of personal choice. Dishes are classified according to the way they are cooked rather than by their main ingredient. At an elaborate dinner six or seven classes may be served. *Mushimono* are steamed foods, of which a favourite is *chawanmushi*, a custard-thick soup garnished with morsels of fish or vegetables. *Yakimono* are grilled foods and the most popular way of cooking fish. The shape of the fish is retained during grilling by threading skewers along its length. They go in and out of the body to give the impression that the fish is swimming. The best yakimono is prepared over glowing charcoal. *Agemono* are deep-fried dishes, of which *tempura* is the best known and loved. The finest tempura is made from a feather-light batter in which the very freshest shellfish, pieces of fish fillet or carefully cut vegetables are dipped. They are then deep-fried at just the right temperature and for just the right time. Golden brown and very hot, the tempura is served with a soya sauce and dipped in a *daikon* (Japanese radish) sauce, and garnished with slices of ginger and perhaps fresh lotus root. *Nimono* is food simmered in

water or some other liquid such as sake. Thin slices of fish or meat are often cooked in this way. Diners pick the food out of the simmering liquid with their chopsticks. The cooking liquor is later supped out of a bowl like a soup. Other classifications are *sashimi*, in which pieces of very fresh raw fish are served with *wasabi*, a green Japanese mustard; *sushi*, vinegared rice patties topped with a variety of foods, particularly raw fish, and *nabe-mono*, which are one-pot meals, such as *sukiyaki*. Most Japanese meals are normally accompanied by *miso* soup and are always served with rice. *Miso-shiru* is a very popular soup, which is also served for breakfast. Its base is a fish stock, made from the *bonito*, which is sold in dried flakes in every food shop in Japan. This stock is then flavoured with miso paste. Floating in the soup are small squares of tofu and strands of seaweed or finely chopped vegetables. In the Japanese manner the soup is slurped with gusto from the bowl while holding back the solid bits with one's chopsticks. Rice is eaten with every meal including breakfast. *Han*, the Japanese word for rice, is given the honourable prefix *go* and rice is referred to as *go-han* (honourable rice). The rice at a meal is usually eaten last rather than as an accompaniment to other foods. The Japanese will eat two or three bowls of it. Strangers to Japanese food do not understand this and sometimes observe that a Japanese meal is not filling. In

FOOD AND DRINK

Some signs are the same everywhere

fact the rice is the core of a meal. Apart from rice, noodles made from buckwheat and wheat flour, the three soya-bean products – *tofu*, *miso* and *shoyu* – and seaweed are the basic Japanese foods.

The Japanese eat noodles almost as often as they do rice. One of the great delights of being in Japan is to eat a bowl of noodles in one of the inexpensive noodle restaurants to be found in even the smallest village. Lean over your bowl and start feeding the noodle strands into your mouth with chopsticks. Once started, you then suck the remaining noodles out of the soup stock in which they are floating. After the noodles are eaten, take the bowl to your mouth and slurp out the residual soup or broth.

Tofu, better known in Chinese restaurants as beancurd, is made by soaking and grinding soya beans. The liquid extracted from the resulting mixture is then curdled. This is pressed into slabs to produce soft-textured delicately flavoured, pale cream tofu. It is sold the day it is prepared.

Miso is made by fermenting soya-bean paste in wooden casks for two or more years. By adding extra ingredients such as barley or wheat grains, different flavours ranging from the mild to the powerful are produced. Miso is rich in vitamins and protein. It is delicious in soups, sauces and marinades and keeps, unrefrigerated, almost indefinitely. Miso is available in the West. Miso soup is particularly nutritious.

Shoyu is Japanese soya sauce, traditionally made from naturally fermented soya beans. It is readily available in Japan and the West. Nowadays, unfortunately, most of the liquid described as soya is really an artifically flavoured cocktail of chemicals. It is best therefore only to buy soya sauce which is clearly labelled 'naturally fermented'.

FOOD AND DRINK

In Japan seaweed as a foodstuff is commonplace, and its use is taken for granted. In fact kombu seaweed is packaged in fancy boxes and given as presents by appreciative guests when they go to dinner. As with land vegetables, the environment of the area in which the seaweed grows affects its quality and taste, but seaweed is usually rich in vitamins and minerals. Apart from its nutritive value, it is very useful as seasoning, and this is the way seaweed is most often used in Japan. *Nori*, *hijiki* and *kombu* are the most common types of seaweed. *Nori* seaweed is dried, pressed into sheets and wrapped around rolls of rice to make *norimaki sushi.* Crumbled over rice or soup, nori adds a distinctive flavour. *Hijiki* is cooked with sauce and eaten as a side dish; it is also good in salads or fried with rice. *Kombu* is best known as a basic constituent of *dashi* or Japanese soup stock, but it can also be used to garnish rice dishes, to

The Japanese love to eat out

season vegetables, and in a variety of other ways.

The main seasoning and condiments used in Japanese cooking are surprisingly few because the cuisine depends as much on the natural flavour of good fresh ingredients, their aroma and their visual beauty as on added flavouring. The main seasonings used, apart from shoyu, miso and seaweed, are *goma*, which is a mixture of toasted and crushed sesame seeds and salt, *mirin* (a sweet fortified wine similar to sherry), ginger root, *togarashi* (a blend of several spices tasting like a combination of black pepper and cayenne), and *wasabi* (a horse-radish mustard).

Japanese Restaurants
A formal meal is very expensive, but while in Japan the opportunity to enjoy the experience at least once should not be missed. Otherwise, you

FOOD AND DRINK

can eat cheaply in Japan in an amazing assortment of restaurants and cafés. Two notes of caution. First, avoid the places in big cities that provide Western-style dishes; they tend to be expensive. Secondly, the Japanese love to eat out and appreciate good food, but they are also happy to pay high prices for an ambience and a location a visitor to the country may not enjoy. Before ordering a meal, always make sure that the price range of a restaurant suits you.

In the restaurant, deciphering a menu and ordering what you want when you cannot read Japanese is greatly simplified by the common practice of displaying very realistic wax models in showcases outside the entrance. The type of bowl or plate which holds the model indicates the national origin of the meal. Large bowls with patterns round the rim are Chinese; plain or delicately patterned bowls or lacquered boxes are Japanese; and flat plates hold European or American dishes.

Once seated in the restaurant you will be given *oshibori*, *o-cha* and *o-hashi*. *Oshibori* are small napkin-sized damp cloths. In cold weather they are hot and in hot weather cold. Use them to wipe your hands and face and then as napkins during the meal. *O-hashi* are chopsticks. At inexpensive places they give you disposable unpainted wooden sticks. These are joined together at the top and to separate them you merely pull one stick away from the other. In better places you are given

lacquered chopsticks. Japanese chopsticks are more pointed, lighter and shorter than the Chinese variety and easier to use. *O-cha*, or green tea, is as much a part of Japanese life as black tea is for the British. It is the common offering in all Japanese restaurants. Tea is given to you when you arrive and at the end of the meal without your requesting it. It is always free. One final point before describing the various types of Japanese eating establishments. On no account blow your nose in a restaurant. This is judged very bad manners. Retreat to the toilet if your nose needs blowing.

Formal Traditional Meals

Ryotei offer traditional Tōkyō- or Kyōto-style full-course dinners. Ryotei are found in *ryokans* (Japanese inns) or as restaurants in their own right. They occupy unidentified premises which from the outside look like traditional Japanese homes. An advance reservation is needed and sometimes a personal introduction as well.

There is an alternative to this style of formal meal and that is a *shojin ryori* dinner. This is a beautifully cooked and presented vegetarian meal served in the dining-room of a Buddhist temple. Again, you will need a reservation. The locations of temples that serve such meals are available from Japanese National Tourist Organization offices. There is a particularly famous one in Tōkyō called Sanko-in Temple which is run by Zen nuns. The abbess, Soei Yoneda, is a very talented cook.

FOOD AND DRINK

Soba-ya (Cheap Noodle Shops)

This is one of the commonest types of restaurants in Japan and one of the cheapest. *Soba-ya* serve four basic kinds of noodles in soup with garnishing on top. *Soba* noodles are long and light brown in colour. They are made from buckwheat flour. *Udon* and *somen* noodles are both made from wheat flour and are white in colour. Udon are long and fat like spaghetti, and somen are long and thin. They are sometimes served ice cold in summer. *Ramen* are the fourth category. They are the more familiar Chinese egg noodles. The Japanese find it very difficult to say 'rrr', so when ordering ramen ask for 'lamen'.

To order in a soba shop, recognised by the noodle dishes in the showcases outside, just stipulate whichever noodles you want. Garnishings vary, but it is easier to take pot luck than to try to specify exactly what you want.

Chuka Ryori-ya (Moderately Priced Chinese Restaurants)

This is a simple Chinese restaurant which a Japanese family might visit for a cheap meal. They sell Japanese versions of regular Chinese dishes.

Koryori-ya (Inexpensive Traditional Restaurants)

Koryori-ya serve a small menu of popular Japanese dishes such as seasonal fresh fish and vegetables. They are also relaxed places in which to drink beer or sake. Koryori-ya are usually small, with a couple of semi-private rooms with tatami mats. They are perfect for a small, intimate, inexpensive

dinner. A *shokuji-dokoro* is a very small version of a koryori-ya, only seating perhaps six to eight people at a few tables in tatami-mat booths. Koryori-ya and shokuji-dokoro are easily recognisable by their traditional Japanese look; they often have unvarnished sliding wooden shutters at the entrance.

Shokudo (Cheap Mixed-Menu Restaurants)

Small and inexpensive, the *shokudo* sell a selection of the most popular Japanese, Western and Chinese dishes. They always display the complete menu of wax models outside. Shokudo are very relaxed and suitable for people travelling on their own. They are popular with students.

Sushi-ya (Moderately Priced Sushi Bar)

Sushi shops are the most atmospheric and distinctive of all small Japanese restaurants. They sell rice delicately seasoned with vinegar, sugar and salt, shaped into rolls, patties, balls and so on. They are topped and filled with slices of raw, boiled or marinated fish, egg omelette, vegetables and seaweed. They also sell *sashimi* (raw fish) on its own.

There are two basic types of sushi: *nigiri*, which originated in Edo, old Tōkyō, and *oshi*, from Osaka. For *nigiri-sushi* the rice is shaped by hand and then a topping is placed on it. For *oshi-sushi* the rice, together with boiled or marinated fish, is packed into wooden moulds of various shapes and sizes and pressed. The block is then cut into smaller sections. The most usual mould is rectangular-shaped, giving square slices of sushi.

The most exciting thing about a sushi bar is that the chef prepares the sushi in front of the customers as it is ordered. The sushi chef is incredibly deft and speedy, and as well as making and serving the sushi he has to remember the cost of each person's assortment of orders. A sushi bar is easily identified by its wax models of rice patties topped with raw fish. Sushi is served either in lacquered boxes or placed on the counter in small saucers. Inside the shop you can sit up at the counter and watch the chef at work, or away from the counter on small tatami mats. The counter is the place where you can most easily choose your selection of sushi. At the side tables the order is normally for a fixed combination tray. In many places they now have a conveyor belt rotating around the counter. On it the chef places an array of different sushi. As they come around the customer chooses what he wants; the price is calculated from the number of saucers at his place when he has finished eating. For the tourist sushi bars are good places to relax and enjoy the food and the Japanese at their best.

Nomi-ya (Snacks and Drinks Bars)

A nomi-ya is a small, basic local bar and can be recognised by the large red lantern hanging outside. Nomi-ya are more for drinking sake and beer than eating, but they do serve snacks. There are no hostesses in nomi-ya, which are relaxing places in which to sit and take time over a drink.

Kissaten (Coffee, Dessert and Snack Shops)

There are many types of kissaten, ranging from the traditional tea-rooms playing Japanese music to modern coffee-shops playing jazz or classical music. They normally have exceptionally good sound systems. The desserts and snacks can be Western or Japanese. Tea or coffee is moderately expensive but once you have bought a cup you are welcome to sit for as long as you wish. Kissaten frequently offer a good breakfast for the price of a coffee, early in the day. This is called 'morning service' in English. Morning service is excellent value and a boon to the tourist on a budget.

O-bento and Ekiben (Meals on Wheels)

O-bento are everyday lunchboxes prepared at home or bought in local shops. Ekiben are train journey lunchboxes. They are sold on train platforms, in and around stations and on express trains.

The boxes themselves are made from thin, unpainted wood or, for the deluxe version, lacquered wood. Inside they divide into neat compartments and contain such foods as sushi rice, grilled chicken, mushrooms, smoked fish, pickled plums, fresh and cooked vegetables. They are sold neatly wrapped in decorative paper and tied with string.

Each area of Japan has its own variety of o-bento and ekiben,

FOOD AND DRINK

containing a particular selection of food and one or two local specialities. At Tōkyō Station there are stands selling ekiben from all over the country, which are delivered fresh four times a day. The Mitsukoshi department store, Ikebukuro branch, Tōkyō, even holds ekiben fairs in November and February when for a week they sell all the popular regional ekiben. For those not travelling by train, o-bento may be purchased from shops in towns and on the main highways at refreshment stops. Special o-bento for celebratory or romantic occasions are available to order in larger cities. For a night out at the theatre it is possible to have a *makunochi*, 'between the curtains', or interval o-bento delivered to the theatre door. A final note of caution. Do not touch the *sando-ichi bento* sold at large stations. They contain regular squares of crustless white bread sandwiches. They are anaemic and tasteless.

Specialities

There are many restaurants in large Japanese cities which specialise in one particular food. The list is too large to mention even a fraction of them, but here are a few different types of food that are usually appreciated by Westerners.

Okonomi-yaki

'Do-it-yourself' restaurants in which the customer makes his own pancakes from a batter and ingredients he has selected. The tables are inlaid with hot plates. Good fun with a party of people. Filling and quite cheap.

Kimono make attractive gifts

Tempura-ya

Foods deep-fried in batter served with a dipping sauce. Moderately expensive.

Sukiyaki-ya

'Do-it-yourself', one-pot meals of various vegetables and thin slices of beef fried at the table. Quite expensive.

Oden

Foods such as tofu cubes, hard-boiled eggs, pressed fishcakes, *daikon*, *konnyaku* and seaweed boiled together in fish stock. Usually sold from street stalls. Unless you ask for something different the vendor will give you a standard combination. Cheap.

Yakitori-ya

Cubes of chicken and chicken liver skewered on bamboo sticks and grilled over charcoal.

SHOPPING

Foreign visitors to Japan can buy tax-free goods in any stores that display a 'Tax-Free' sign. Most major department stores, hotel arcades, and specialist shops in tourist areas offer this facility. Savings range between 5 to 40 per cent. You will need to take your passport with you to the shop and export forms detailing the goods you have bought will be attached to it. Customs on the way out may wish to see the goods to make sure you didn't buy them, for example, for a Japanese friend. Electrical goods, cameras, watches and precious stones are the types of items normally on offer. In large cities similar goods may also be bought in discount stores at similarly reduced prices or even lower. See listings under **Tōkyō** and **Osaka** for addresses. For present or souvenir buying it is best to go to a department store (*depāto*). This will save you a lot of walking about, and the vast range of merchandise will also give you plenty of ideas. The stores are self-contained worlds in which all human needs from baby clothes to funeral arrangements are politely and enthusiastically looked after. Each department store has a particular style and price range. Choose the medium to cheap stores, the service and the goods will still be of an excellent standard. Particular stores are listed in the **What to See** sections. Japanese pottery, lacquerware, dolls, *cloisonné* (fine wire is patterned onto a metal base and the spaces filled with a fired glass finish), kitchen knives and paper goods are some suggestions for presents. However, you will be overwhelmed with choice, and this will be the problem rather than finding something you want to buy.

ACCOMMODATION

There is no shortage of accommodation for the traveller in Japan. In the cities there is a wide variety of options and in rural areas there are small hotels, *minshuku* (a Japanese version of bed and breakfast), temples which take visitors, and sometimes *ryokans* (traditional Japanese hotels or inns), French-style pensions, or People's Lodges (guest house-like accommodation). Much could be written on the subject, but for the short-term visitor matters can be simplified.

The service in Japan's major hotels is invariably first class and expensive. Those with particular character or other merits are listed in the **What To See** sections. If you are visiting Japan as part of an arranged trip or for business reasons, your travel agent will book you into a vetted hotel. Some offer Japanese as well as Western-type rooms, and if you want a room with tatami-mat floor and sunken bath tub, request a reservation in a Japanese-style room. For the independent traveller your choice of hotel will depend on your budget. They range from the international luxury type to the business hotel to the cheap but clean, small, local establishments. Avec or love hotels are discussed later (see page 99).

ACCOMMODATION

Youth Hostels

The very cheapest places to stay are youth hostels. There are quite a number in Japan and their rules and regulations are similar to those in the West. Details and addresses in Japan are available in a booklet from the YHA head office of your own country, and some are listed in the **What To See** sections. Youth hostels are convenient for one-night stays, but at busy holiday times they are popular and heavily used and need to be booked ahead.

Ryokans (Japanese Inns)

These provide the very best of traditional Japanese taste, culture and food. They are usually sited in a beautiful spot and/or look onto elegant gardens. The service will be restrained and flawless in its maintenance of correct behaviour.

Ryokans are very expensive but worth at least one night's stay for the experience. A certain style of behaviour is expected from their

Ryokan: comfort and restraint

guests, but allowances are made for foreigners. A small booklet, *Japan Ryokan Guide*, is obtainable from a JNTO office abroad or in Japan.

Minshuku

These are definitely the best places to stay for independent visitors to Japan who are on a budget but who do not have to be extremely careful. Minshuku are family homes that take guests and staying in one really gives an insight into and feel of Japanese life. They provide a room, bedding, breakfast and supper. Foreigners are a novelty and you will be treated with real hospitality and warmth by your hosts once you have established that you are sensitive to and respect and understand the simpler of their customs. The most important of these are to remember to leave your shoes at the door and not to use soap in the hot tub. Others you can learn as you go along by being careful and observant as you move around.

Addresses and reservations for minshuku can be obtained from the information counters found at most reasonably-sized railway stations. A detailed list of addresses and minshuku customs can be obtained from the Japan Minshuku Association, Pearl Building, Room 201, 10–8 Kyakunincho 2-chome, Shinjuku, Tōkyō (tel: (03) 3371-8120). The word minshuku is pronounced 'minsh-ku'.

Business Hotels

Straightforward, no-frills accommodation in clean, efficiently run hotels. Rooms are small but well equipped and the hotel provides facilities such as fax and photocopying machines. Food (except in vending machines) and room service are not always available. The cost is less than a major hotel but more than a Japanese inn (see below). Business hotels are usually located near or in city centres for ease of access to railway and subway stations.

Japanese Inn

This is a cheap version of a ryokan (see page 98) and recommended if you are on a budget and wish to experience traditional Japanese customs and lifestyle. The rooms are tatami (straw matted), divided by paper screens and sparsely but tastefully decorated. Meals are an optional extra.

Japanese inns are normally good value and provide an excellent introduction to Japanese home cooking.

Love Hotels

Because most Japanese live in very small houses or apartments with their families, it is very hard for young unmarried or even married couples to find somewhere to make love privately and out of earshot of other people. The problem also arises for people carrying on affairs which they want to keep secret from family and neighbours. The solution society has found is short-stay hotels, called love hotels or avec hotels. Such establishments are quite common and their advertisements giving the rates for a 'rest' per hour and details of facilities offered are to be seen in most large cities. The adverts are garish but the hotels themselves are run very discreetly. They are normally surrounded by a high wall and the entrance and exit are separate to reduce the chance of embarrassing encounters. The anonymity of the guests is closely guarded, but the management tries to offer all the facilities needed to allow them to indulge in their wildest fantasies. Even the 'straight' rooms are decorated in sensuous style with lots of satin, soft cushions and mirrors. Videos with pornographic films are also common nowadays, and cameras are available so that guests can film themselves. A tip for travellers on a budget: after 22.00 hrs the room rates at love hotels are often lower than those of regular hotels. So if exotic surroundings do not put you off sleeping, they make a cheap alternative for a single night's stay.

CULTURE, ENTERTAINMENT AND NIGHTLIFE

CULTURE, ENTERTAINMENT AND NIGHTLIFE

The Japanese have a rich and varied cultural history, and classical performing arts such as *Noh* and *Kabuki* and the elegant pleasures of pastimes such as the tea ceremony continue to be appreciated and to flourish.

Culture
Noh Theatre
Noh is a stylized dance drama performed to the accompaniment of music and singing. The stage is stark and the actors wear masks and gorgeous elaborate costumes. Movement is slow and the storyline is conveyed by a symbolism difficult to understand without some background knowledge. It is not easily appreciated by a foreigner. However, it is worth a visit for the

Traditional stylised comedy

spectacle and an insight into the contemplative nature of traditional Japanese arts. Noh plays may be seen at:
Kongo Noh Stage, Muromachi, Shijo-Agaru, Nakagyo-ku, Kyōto (tel: (075) 221-3049).
Performances every fourth Sunday in the month except August.
Ginza Noh Stage, 5–15 Ginza 6-chome, Chūō-ku, Tōkyō (tel: (03) 3571-0197).

Kabuki
Kabuki features only male actors, who play both male and female roles. They wear traditional costume and the plays depict either the lives of ordinary people, or those of the noble classes, in a Japan of earlier times. The dialogue and gestures used to convey the

stories are formalised but there is an energy, colour and accessibility in Kabuki missing from Noh theatre and foreigners often enjoy performances. English-language programmes are normally available. Kabuki may be seen at:

Minamiza Theatre, Shijo Ohashi Tamato, Higashiyama-ku, Kyōto (tel: (075) 561-1155).

Shin Kabuki-za, 5–59 Namba Shinchi, Minami-ku, Osaka (tel: (06) 631-2121).

Kabuki-za, 4–3 Ginza-Higashi, Chūō-ku, Tōkyō (tel: (03) 3541-3131).

Bunraku

Bunraku (puppet theatre) is the third Japanese classical form. The main character puppets are manipulated by as many as three puppeteers and they are very lifelike. The stories told are similar to the tales unfolded in Kabuki. The scripts are traditional and usually well known by the audience. Osaka is considered the birthplace and capital of Bunraku theatre, although first-class performances are also given in theatres in Tōkyō and Kyōto. Bunraku may be seen at:

Kyōto Gion Corner, Yasaka-Kaikan, Higashiyama-ku, Kyōto (tel: (075) 561-1155).

National Bunraku Theatre, 1–12–10 Nihombashi, Chūō-ku, Osaka (tel: (06) 212-2531).

Tōkyō National Theatre, 1–4 Hayabusacho, Chiyoda-ku, Tōkyō (tel: (03) 3265-7411).

Entertainment and Nightlife

The Japanese spend more time outside the home than in it, and a wide variety of meeting and entertaining places such as coffee-shops, tea-houses, restaurants, bars and cocktail lounges are an integral part of even a small Japanese town. Cinemas, discotheques and intimate clubs are to be found in downtown areas alongside 'Soapland' districts where striptease and massage parlours rub shoulders with street-food kiosks and fast-food restaurants. Prices in restaurants and bars vary widely and they are usually high in establishments that do not display a price list. The cost of drinks in any bar is much higher than you would pay at home, and in those that employ hostesses to fill your glass and make idle chat they can be very expensive. The Japanese do not entertain at home, and if they invite you out they will expect to pick up the bill just as though you were a house-guest for dinner. Japanese coffee-shops pride themselves on serving exquisite coffee and on providing a first-class sound system. A cup of coffee is expensive, but once you have ordered you can sit for as long as you wish, look at the magazines and comics (always available), and listen to good jazz, classical music, or whatever is the shop's speciality. Entertainment areas are busy from early evening and 'Soapland' districts start to get lively from 21.00 hrs onwards. Some bars and clubs stay open until the very early hours. Paid-for sex is expensive in Japan and prices rise rapidly as the customer's requirements move from a 'basic massage' to more exotic services. In Tōkyō and Osaka there are also 'Adonis' bars for women.

WEATHER

WEATHER AND WHEN TO GO

Climate

Japan has four distinct seasons. Spring begins in March (early April in northern Honshū and Hokkaidō) and lasts until the beginning of June. April and May are warm and dry months, good for travelling. Late March to mid-April the cherry blossom ripens northwards from Kyūshū to Hokkaidō ('The Cherry Blossom Frontier'). Summer and a rainy season starts early June. It is hot and a time of high humidity (except in Hokkaidō). From mid-July to early September it remains hot but not wet. Mountain areas are refreshing at this time of the year. Autumn is a time of clear skies and comfortable temperatures although late September can be wet. Winter in the north and at high altitudes is cold, snow covered and beautiful. In other areas temperatures rarely drop below freezing.

Clothes

For spring and autumn you will need a warm sweater. Summer is hot and humid, and light, cotton clothes are the most practical. In the winter one light and one thick sweater will be needed and a waterproof coat. An umbrella is useful.

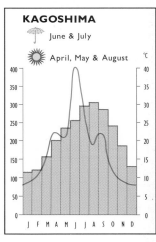

KAGOSHIMA
June & July
April, May & August

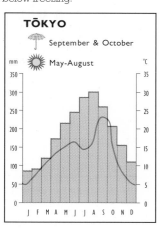

TŌKYO
September & October
May-August

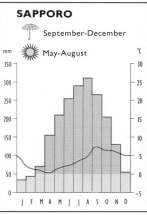

SAPPORO
September-December
May-August

HOW TO BE A LOCAL

The Japanese will not expect you to know their customs or speak their language, but they will really appreciate and enjoy it if you make the effort to learn a few key phrases and show that you are available to learn some of their traditional etiquette and manners. Footwear and bathing are usually the first two areas of Japanese life that may confuse foreigners and thus embarrass their hosts.

Shoes

In Japanese homes, and some places such as temples, small hotels and some restaurants there are rituals attached to the wearing of shoes that need to be observed. On entering a home you leave your shoes in the hall which is at a lower level than the house proper, you then step up into the house and into a pair of slippers that will be placed out for the family and visitors. You wear these unless you are invited to enter a room laid out with tatami mats (closely woven straw flooring). At the entrance to such a room you leave your slippers at the door and proceed in your stockinged feet. At the entrance to the toilet you change your slippers for another pair (sometimes marked WC on the toe). Change back when you leave the toilet. Never go barefoot.

Bathing

The Japanese do not wash in the same water they bathe in and find it perplexing that we do. For bathing you will be given a small towel and a cotton dressing gown (*yukata*). Undress in the space provided outside the bathroom. Take the small towel in with you. Squat on the low stool you will find outside the hot tub and scoop water out of the tub over yourself with the small bowl provided, or alternatively, use the shower that will be set into the wall at knee height. Soap up the towel and use it to wash yourself then shampoo, shave and so on. Finally shower or scoop water from the tub to rinse off all the soap and rinse out the towel. Now sit in the tub, soak and relax. Once out of the tub wring out the towel and dry yourself with it. Put on your underclothes and then the *yukata*. You have finished and the tub is ready for the next person.

Bowing

The Japanese bow a lot to each other on meeting or departing. The depth and frequency of the bows depends on the status of the people involved. As a foreigner you will automatically be accorded high status, but to be on the safe side imitate any bows you receive and you will then be sure of not offending anyone. To bow you leave both arms straight and bow with the upper body. Shaking hands is an alternative way of introducing yourself and a novelty to the Japanese. However, a strong handshake is not needed and would not be understood.

Gifts

Gift-giving is an important part of Japanese life and ritual. Meeting for dinner at a friend's house, saying goodbye, meeting someone important for the first time, thanking someone for their help or a service provided, and a myraid other occasions are all times when giving or receiving gifts may be appropriate. Before leaving home buy a number of small lightweight gifts. Presents with some characteristic of your home country will be especially appreciated. Incidentally Scotch whisky, especially Johnny Walker Black Label, is a very prestigious gift for a man. Always wrap your gifts and do not press the recipient to open it while you are there. As with much else in Japanese life there are many subtleties to present-giving that you will not understand, but the one golden rule to remember in this situation and others is that neither party should be embarrassed or lose face.

Toilets

Japanese toilets are of the squat variety. There is a hood at one end and this is the direction you face. Carry toilet paper with you since some public lavatories do not supply it. The cistern for flushing is filled through a tap which issues water into a sink set over the cistern. Wash your hands under this tap. This ingenious method saves water. If you do not like 'squatting' toilets, more and more Western-style models are now provided, especially in large hotels and big cities. Some public toilets are used by both men and women, and it is quite normal for a woman to walk past a man's urinal on her way to a cubicle.

Colds

It is normal to clear your throat or sniff if you have a cold or a running nose (and even acceptable to spit discreetly in the street). However, it is not done to blow your nose in public. The people you see wearing masks over the mouth and nose do so because they have a cold, not because of pollution. Go to the toilet or a private place if you need to blow your nose.

Quick Tips

● The Japanese are prepared to be very helpful to foreigners but they do not like criticism. If you do say something critical, preface it with constructive praise first.

● Well-known tourist sites are very popular with the Japanese. If possible, travel midweek and rest or visit less well-known places at weekends. In this way you will miss the crowds.

● Buy a Japanese phrase book and learn a few useful phrases. Pronunciation is not difficult and once you try a few words the Japanese lose their shyness and try out their English.

● If asking somebody for directions or other help, choose a young to middle-aged man or woman or a teenage boy. Old people are often shy of foreigners and teenage girls are often self-conscious with them. They become tongue-tied and shrink into the cover of their friends if approached by one.

● Do not worry more than sensibly about the safety of your property or person.

● Any transaction you may have in a hotel, shop, taxi etc, will be straightforward. Do not haggle or tip; neither would be either expected or understood.

Restaurants

At a Japanese restaurant you will be given a small hot towel before the meal. This is initially used to wipe your hands and refresh your face, and then as the meal proceeds to wipe your fingers as needed. Before a meal everyone says *itadakimas* ('good health') before they start and *gochiso-sama-deshita* ('thank you it was a feast') at the end.

Alcohol

The Japanese do like alcoholic drinks and there is no shame in getting somewhat drunk. In fact, in some circumstances the hosts expect you to drink too much. However, this is a Japanese custom that you should feel free to ignore, even at the risk of hurting someone's feelings. Beer and/or sake are the usual accompaniments to a meal. You do not pour your own drinks but allow someone else to do it just as you will pour theirs. An empty cup or glass is a signal that you would like a fill up.

Finding an Address

It is extremely difficult even for local people and taxi-drivers to find a place in Japan just by its address. This is because there is no logical system of house numbers or street or road names. In fact until the middle of the 1950s houses were numbered by the chronological order in which they were built, not by their location. In many areas houses numbered before the system changed still retain their old numbers, so complicating any new scheme of numbers. Streets do not have names, although some major roads and avenues do; instead, addresses are by district, and within each district each building has a one-or two-digit (hyphenated) number. The smallest district unit is called a *chome*, and the largest district unit is called a *ku*. Between these two are other units of varying size. Sometimes they are called

One way of getting from A to B

HOW TO BE A LOCAL

cho or *machi*. Cities are suffixed by *shi*, and prefectures by *ken*. This is helpful in distinguishing a city from a prefecture when they have the same name. A Western example is New York City and New York State. Rural addresses may contain the word *mura*, which means 'village', and *gun* which is a county, a unit smaller than a prefecture.

The best way to locate an address is to find it on a map of the vicinity. This is made easier by the practice of printing small maps on the back of business cards, restaurant match-packets and such like. Otherwise, for a first visit to a place, travel to the general vicinity by bus or train and then take a cab for the last part of the journey.

Sex

The Japanese believe that we have two souls, one that is spiritual and another that is earthbound and pleasure seeking. Both need nourishment and within this context male and female sexuality have been equally celebrated in Japan although the emphasis in the past has been on female demureness and male boldness and passion.

In every reasonably sized town there is an entertainment area (or 'Soap' district, named after the practice in massage parlours of the 'hostess' soaping herself before massaging the client with her body) where men go to drink and visit striptease and massage parlours. In large towns such areas expand to include coffee-shops, discothéques, cinemas and wine bars and they are just

as widely visited by women as men. For men who wish to visit sex establishments it is important not to confuse them with ordinary bars where a hostess will serve and pour your drinks and try to make conversation. In these places you pay extra for the drinks but no extras are supplied by the hostess. In such places expect your bill to be measured in tens of pounds or twenty-dollar bills. In massage parlours or other establisments where sex is available costs are very high and can be measured in hundreds of pounds/dollars.

Dating

Western men dating Japanese women is a more common occurrence in Japan than vice versa but either way around is socially acceptable. Whether the relationship is platonic or not depends upon the individuals and there is no general rule. Public displays of affection are embarrassing for the Japanese. Holding hands is about as far as you should go.

If you are hoping for a sexual liaison in Japan or just wish to be on the safe side, then it would be sensible for you, male or female, to take condoms with you. Contraceptive pills are not generally available and Japanese condoms are said to be too small for *gaijin*. Just in case you are desperate Japanese condoms are packed in boxes, chocolate style and they are called 'skinless skins' in 'English' or *boshi* (hats) in slang. Many English words or phrases have found their way directly into the Japanese language.

CHILDREN

Children are well catered for in Japan and there are theme parks, aquariums, zoos, video display exhibitions and other child-orientated events readily available up and down the country. There is also a Disney World on the outskirts of Tōkyō and the Tobu World Square (scale models of famous world monuments) north of Tōkyō at Kinugawa. Local tourist information offices will have full details of their area's amenities. On a broader note, children in Japan are not at any statistical risk from molesters or other criminals and they are allowed to walk, cycle and travel on public transport on their own from a very early age. Family homes and schools are still found in city centres and at either end of the day one can see children of all ages in the middle of town on subways, buses, cycle paths and in shops.

Creeping unwillingly to school?

Japanese children really enjoy meeting foreign boys and girls and later becoming penfriends, and if you do take children with you to Japan they will have no difficulty in making friends despite language differences.

TIGHT BUDGET

Japan is an expensive country but there are ways of maintaining a tight budget and it is possible to keep expenses equivalent to those you would expect in Britain or America. The first essential if you plan to do a lot of travelling is to buy a Japan Rail Pass before leaving your own country. This will allow you to travel freely on all JR rail lines (except the 'Nozomi' Shinkansen train), buses and ferries.
Even cheap accommodation in

TIGHT BUDGET

Food stalls: good for tight budgets

Japan is clean and respectable so do not be put off a place by its low cost. *Minshuku* (Japanese bed, dinner and breakfast) and Japanese inns offer the best value plus an authentic experience of ordinary Japanese life. Youth hostels are also cheap and clean. They tend to be very busy during holiday periods. For breakfast, if it is not included in accommodation costs, choose a coffee shop and order 'Morning Service' in English. This is available until 11.00 hrs, and for the price of a coffee you will receive coffee, toast, a boiled egg and salad or similar.

For the Japanese, eating out is just as common as eating at home and there are restaurants to suit every taste and pocket. Noodle shops and stalls, especially those at railway stations, offer filling and well-prepared bowls of noodles with topping. Wax models showing exactly what you will receive and the prices are displayed in these establishments and most other eating houses.

The prices of fruit and vegetables are to a great degree determined by the perfection of their appearance. Slightly marked or deformed specimens are sold cheaply. They are put together in a bowl and sold off as a unit.

Quick Tips

● Western-style foods such as bread, cheese and cakes are more expensive than traditional Japanese foods.

● Never order a meal before knowing the cost, only the most expensive restaurants do not display prices.

● Alcohol is expensive, sometimes exorbitantly so, in Japanese bars and clubs. If you are on a budget and would like a drink it is best to buy from a supermarket or slot machine and drink it in your hotel room.

● For snacking or self-catering, buy the made-up lunchboxes (*o-bento*) of rice, pickles, fishcake and so on, sold in grocery shops.

● Finally, one or other of the many chains of hamburger bars are always involved in a trade war with a competitor. Look out for their special offers.

FESTIVALS, EVENTS AND PUBLIC HOLIDAYS

The Japanese have a great many festivals and every town and village seems to have its own calendar of events. Historical costumes, music and ritual play an important role in many of them and they help to maintain and sustain the rich texture of traditional Japanese culture. Most have some kind of religious significance, but they are normally boisterous affairs with lots of merry-making, sake drinking and spectator participation. The TIC offices in Tōkyō and Kyōto publish a monthly programme of festivals and similar events. If you plan to visit a town or district for the period of a particular festival make sure you book accommodation and transport in advance since these events are always popular.

Apart from regional festive holidays, there are thirteen national holidays celebrated in Japan. If they occur on a Sunday then the following Monday also becomes a public holiday. On such days banks and government offices are closed, but hotels, large department stores and restaurants stay open. They are listed here, followed by details of some of the most popular festivals.

National Holidays

1 January–New Year's Day (only 1 January is an official holiday, but government offices and factories are closed from 29 December to 3 January)
15 January–Adults' Day
11 February–Founding of the Nation Day
20 or 21 March–Vernal Equinox Day
29 April–Greenery Day
3 May–Constitution Day
5 May–Children's Day (most Japanese take a long break at this time, combining these three holidays with the weekends before and after them. The period from 29 April to 6 May, called 'Golden Week', is essentially a national week off. This is not a good time to travel.)
15 September–Respect for the Aged Day
23 or 24 September–Autumn Equinox Day
10 October–Health-Sports Day
3 November–Culture Day
23 November–Labour Thanksgiving Day
23 December–Emperor's Birthday

Summer
13–15 July (August in some areas): O-Bon

At this time of the year the Japanese like to return to their home towns or villages to take part in the *O-Bon* ceremonies that mark the return to earth of all departed ancestors. At the end of the rituals, to mark the return of the spirits to their own world, lightened paper lanterns are set to float down rivers and out to sea. Yasukuni Shrine in Tōkyō and Nachi Shrine in Katsuura, Wakaywama Prefecture hold large ceremonies.

17 July: Gion Matsuri

This is perhaps the best known of all Japanese festivals. It takes place in Kyōto, and events span a month. The highlight is a huge procession of floats on 17 July. The ceremony is over 1000 years old and began as a

FESTIVALS

purification ritual to rid the city of plague. Each of Kyōto's 29 neighbourhoods builds its own elaborately decorated float.

23–25 July: Soma-Nomaoi

The Wild Horse Festival is held in Haramachi, in Fukushima Prefecture. One thousand horsemen in traditional costume try to catch ceremonial flags which are fired into the air above them. Other men on foot attempt to catch and ride one of a herd of corraled wild horses.

2–7 August: Nebuta Matsuri

This is the main festival of Aomori Prefecture in northern Honshū. At the finale, huge and spectacular papier maché figures are carried through the streets of Aomori City.

Autumn
7–9 October: Okunchi

Held at the Suwa Shrine in Nagasaki, the Festival celebrates the city's ancient links with China and, more recently, the Dutch. Lion and snake dances, firecrackers and Japanese in baggy Dutch pantaloons contribute to the fun.

22 October: Kurama-No-Iti-Matsuri

The Fire Festival of Kurama takes place in Sakyo-ku in Kyōto. The main event is a long procession of people carrying lighted torches to the gate of Yuki Shrine. They pass between rows of bonfires placed along the roadsides.

22 October: Jidai Matsuri

The Heian Shrine in Kyōto is the start of a large procession to mark the founding of the city. Thousands of people dressed in the costumes of each era march along in a noisy, happy event.

15 November: Shichi-go-san

On this day 3, 5 and 7 year old children are dressed in their best clothes and taken to shrines or temples where prayers are given for their good health.

Winter
31 December/1 January: Joya-No-Kane and Ganjtsu

On New Year's Eve everybody stays up until midnight to celebrate the coming of the new year. Temple bells ring out 108 times from the stroke of 24.00 hrs. New Year's Day is seen as an opportunity for renewal and a fresh start. Debts are paid and arguments settled. Festivities go on for seven days and most businesses come to a halt. On 2 January the Imperial Family appears at the Imperial Palace in Tōkyō and huge crowds gather to take part.

3 or 4 February: Setsubun

Commemorating the last day of winter according to the lunar calendar, this festival is held at all major temples throughout the country. The main attraction is bean throwing, when the temple priests or celebrities such as sumo wrestlers throw handfuls of beans to the crowd who chant in unison: 'in with good luck, out with devils'.

5–11 February: Yuki Matsuri (Snow Festival)

The Snow Festival of Sapporo in Hokkaidō was started in 1950. The main feature of the festival is a competition of spectacular ice sculptures. These are exhibited in Odori Park near the

Spectacle is part of life in Japan

city centre, on the second weekend in February. A different theme is chosen each year, and the sculptures are usually very large, intricately carved, and true to life.

Third Saturday in February: Eyo

Eyo, or *Hadaka Matsuri*, is one of a series of purification, or 'naked' festivals held at this time of the year in many parts of Japan. At Saidaji Temple in Saidaji, Okayama Prefecture, hundreds of young men dressed only in loin cloths immerse themselves after dark in the Yoshii River. They then gather in the temple grounds and from a high window a priest throws down two special sticks or wands which the men scramble frantically to retrieve and return to him. The struggle is ferocious since the two people who are successful in returning the wands are guaranteed a year of good fortune.

Spring
1–14 March: Omizutori
The water-drawing ceremony of Todaiji Temple, Nara, includes monks dancing with flaming torches. Water is then drawn from a secret well and dedicated to Buddha to mark the start of spring.

5–8 April: Kagura-sai
Held at the Ise Shrines in Ise. Shinto music and dances and Noh plays are performed at the Grand Shrines. Around 8 April, Buddha's birthday is celebrated throughout Japan with services at most temples.

FESTIVALS

29 April and 3 May: Hata-Age

Teams of people fly huge kites from the tops of the hills that surround the city of Nagasaki. There is also a big kite festival (*Odako-Age*) on 3 and 5 May on the beach at Nakatajima near Hamamatsu, Shizuoka Prefecture.

30 April: Cherry Blossom

Cherry Blossom celebrations with festivities all over Japan. Cherry Blossom-viewing parties are held at different times up and down the county depending on the ripening date of the blossom. Local television weather forecasts give updates on the state of the blossom ripeness.

5 May: Kodomo-No-Hi (Children's Day)

This national holiday centres around all of the nation's children, but with a special emphasis on young boys. It is sometimes known as Boys' Day. At this time families fly giant paper *koi* (carp) from their homes. The *koi* symbolises the strength of manhood, the largest representing the eldest son and the increasing smaller ones the younger children.

15 May: Aoi Matsuri

The *aoi*, or hollyhock, is thought to be efficacious in rituals aimed at preventing hurricanes and earthquakes. This is a very old Kyōto festival and is said to date back to the 6th century. A long procession of many hundreds of people in beautiful traditional court costume walk from the old imperial palace to two Shinto shrines where religious ceremonies are performed.

The White Heron Dance is performed each October at Tōkyō's Asakusa Kannon Temple to celebrate the Meiji Restoration

SPORT

Sumo

Sumo is Japan's national sport and part of the country's cultural fabric. Top sumo wrestlers have the status and riches of Hollywood stars, but they are also treated with a deference and respect normally only accorded to royalty.

There are six grand sumo tournaments held each year. They last 15 days and at each one all the sumo stables compete against each other. These events are great community occasions and whole families will turn up with packed lunches, drinks and cushions to spend all day at the stadium. The sumo ring is made of clay and marked off by a half-buried straw rope. Two wrestlers meet in the ring. Once there, the wrestlers loosen up with a movement called *shiko*. They raise, in turn, each leg sideways to waist height, bring it down to the ground and simultaneously slap their thighs. The fight, once started, is over quickly. The techniques are executed with such speed that one needs to be alert to see them. The wrestlers move with consummate skill and their expertise can easily be misjudged by a casual observer. The rules are simple. The first wrestler to set a foot or any other part of his body outside the ring, or to touch the ground inside the ring with anything but the sole of his foot, is the loser. There is no classification by weight. The lighter men try to overcome their weight handicap by making use of their superior speed and agility. Ranking is based on a pyramid system, with teenage beginners (*jonokuchi*) at the bottom and grand champions (*yokozuna*) at the top. Juniors, surprisingly, start their training with the same build as ordinary mortals. They then put on weight by eating large quantities of rice with each meal. The lifestyle in a sumo stable is strict and dictated by the stable master.

Sumo is steeped in tradition and ritual, but it is equally about professionalism and winning. Of the many hundreds of wrestlers few become nationally known. Competition is fierce and Western attitudes to sport are beginning to influence age-old traditions. Even the legendary inscrutability of the competitors has now been breached. Nowadays winners sometimes allow themselves a smile of victory and losers a frown in defeat. The rigorous discipline of a sumo wrestler's training deters most foreigners from joining their ranks.

Sumo tournaments

There are six tournaments a year, each lasting 15 days. These are held in January, May and September in Tōkyō; in March in Osaka; July in Nagoya; November in Fukuoka.

Tōkyō–Kokugikan Sumo Hall (tel: (03) 3623-5111).
Osaka–Osaka Furitsu Taiikukaikan (tel: (06) 631-0120).
Nagoya–Aichi Ken Taiikukan (tel: (052) 271-0001).
Fukuoka–Fukuoka Kokusai Center Sogo Hall (tel: (092) 291-9311).

There is a **Museum of Sumo** based at 1–3–28, Yokoami, Sumida-ku, Tōkyō (*open:* 09.30–16.30 hrs, weekdays).

SPORT

Clash of the Sumo Titans

Baseball

Baseball is loved by the Japanese. During the season almost any evening's television will include 3 or 4 hours of baseball on one or more channels. Most schools, universities and companies field their own teams, and a day at the ball-park complete with coca cola and hot dogs is a popular way to spend a Saturday or Sunday. There are only six professional teams, but the spring and summer tournaments between the best of the high-school teams also receive national attention. The professional season runs from April to October, and the main stadiums are Jingu and Korakuen in Tōkyō, Missei in Osaka and Koshien in Kobe.

Golf

Next to sumo and baseball, golf is the great Japanese sporting passion. However, because of the shortage of courses it is also the most expensive of popular pastimes. To obtain membership of the top clubs requires an outlay of the equivalent of hundreds or thousands of pounds/dollars and the necessary social and political connections. As a visitor to Japan you will probably only get a chance to play if you are invited to do so by a Japanese business colleague or friend. A round of golf is considered a perfectly legitimate occasion for discussing even the highest levels of business.

The high, green net constructions you may see from train windows or rising above downtown apartment blocks or department stores are golf driving ranges. They provide both practice facilities and a substitute for the real thing for those who cannot afford membership of a golf club.

DIRECTORY

Contents

Arriving

Getting There

Pex return fares are the simplest and most straightforward way of booking moderately economic flights to Japan. The main drawbacks with them are that you have to decide in advance exactly when you are going and coming back and no stopovers are allowed. Most travel agents can find you cheaper fares than Pex with the more obscure airlines. They are perfectly all right, but the journey may take longer because of idiosyncratic flight patterns and stopovers in unlikely places. The tickets are cheaper, but otherwise suffer the same disadvantages as Pex. Regular scheduled tickets allow late booking, open-dated return and some stopovers, but they are expensive and in many cases more than a 'Round-the-World' fare. Different airlines combine to produce 'Round-the-World' tickets and they give you a variety of possible routes. The only condition is that you continue to travel round the world in one direction only. This does not matter if you are going to Japan since it is almost as far to Europe or the East Coast of America whether you fly east or west. With the 'Round-the-World' ticket you can plan your own itinerary and stop off for a few days or more at exotic places *en route*. This makes the price of the ticket seem much more reasonable. Different airlines have different rules, but with most you can change your flight dates and routes three or four times *en route* without incurring any extra charge.

Visa/Inoculation

Most residents of European countries do not need a visa to visit Japan and they may stay for up to 90 or 180 days without applying for one (residents of the UK can stay up to 180 days). Visitors from the US, Canada and New Zealand, will need a visa only for visits of over 90 days; they are readily given and are free of charge. Apply to the Japanese Embassy in your country for details and check requirements before you leave. Visitors from Australia need a visa for any visit to Japan. Visitors from Europe, Australia or America do not need any special inoculation certificates to get into Japan. Once there, you do not need to take any health precautions that you would not take at home.

Going to and from the Airport

Narita (also called New Tōkyō International Airport), 40 miles (65 km) from downtown Tōkyō, is the departure and arrival point for international flights. A second terminal was added in 1993 and there are plans for a further two runways. Haneda Airport is for domestic flights. The best ways to get to and from the airport are by travelling on a bus or train. Do not take a taxi unless you are very rich or travelling on somebody else's money. The Airport Limousine Bus information and ticket office is found in the Arrival Hall just outside the exit from the Customs Hall. There are limousine bus (just regular coaches but called limousine for some reason) services to Tōkyō City Air Terminal (TCAT), Tōkyō Station and all the major hotels (the coach goes from one hotel to the next in a circular route). Another service, the Airport Shuttle Bus, links Narita with leading hotels in Tōkyō. Depending on the traffic the journey can take between one and a half and two hours. For travel back to the airport you need to get the bus at least three hours before plane departure time. If you leave from TCAT you can book in for your flight and hand your luggage in. It will be taken to the airport and put on your flight. This is a great service and allows you to enjoy your time at Narita.

The Keisei Skyliner is a privately operated express train between Narita Airport and Keisei-Ueno Station in Tōkyō. It runs every 40 minutes between 06.00 and 20.00hrs, and takes exactly an hour. From Keisei-Ueno Station you can take a taxi or subway (not recommended for your first visit) to your destination. There is a shuttle bus from the Arrival Hall at the airport to the Keisei-Narita Airport Station, which is a short distance away. The Keisei Information Counter and ticket office is near the exit from the Customs Hall. You will have to pay an airport tax on departure from Narita. Buy a ticket at TCAT or at a tax counter at the airport (before entering the departure lounge).

Osaka's futuristic new Kansai International Airport, opened in September 1994, is Japan's second largest airport and operates international and domestic flights. From here there is no airport tax payable.

Camping

There are some campsites in Japan, but they tend to be difficult to find and primitive. Camping is not a popular or common pastime. People on a tight budget would be better advised to stay in youth hostels. **Japan Youth Hostels** is at Hoken Kaikan, Sadohara-cho, Ichigaya Shinjuku-ku, Tōkyō 162 (tel: (03) 3269-5831).

Chemist (see Pharmacies)

Customs Regulations

The following items may be taken into Japan duty free (tobacco and alcohol, only those aged 20 or over).

- 400 cigarettes or 100 cigars or 500g tobacco
- 3 normal-sized bottles of alcoholic drink
- 50g perfume
- souvenirs to the total value of 200,000 yen.

Pornography and illegal drugs are *not* allowed. Penalties for drug-carrying are severe.

Disabled

In large cities many lavatories provide special facilities, and some hotels can provide rooms designed for the disabled. Pedestrian crossings broadcast birdsong to help the blind know when to cross.

With advance warning help is available for disabled passengers at Narita International Airport, where there are adapted toilet facilities.

The Airport Limousine Bus (see page 116) is accessible to disabled passengers. Wheelchair hire is available from Japan Abilities Incorporated, 5–16–4, Yoyogi, Shibiya-ku, Tōkyō (tel: (03) 3460).

Some hotels in Tōkyō have facilities for the disabled. Among them are the Imperial Hotel, The New Otani, Tōkyō Prince Hotel and Miyako Hotel.

Driving (see Transport)

Electricity

From Tōkyō east to Hokkaidō the current is 100 volts at 50 cycles. Western Japan operates on 100 volts at 60 cycles. North Americans with electrical equipment that operates at 110volts/60 cycles will have no problems. Europeans using appliances designed to operate at 240volts/50 cycles will need to adjust them or, if not convertible they will simply operate at a lower capacity. An adapter plug is required for European devices. Some of the major hotels have 220volt/50cycle outputs.

Embassies and Consulates (In Tōkyō)

Australia: 2–1–14, Mita, Minato-ku (tel: (03) 3453-0251)
Canada: 7–3–38, Akasaka, Minato-ku (tel: (03) 3408-2101)
Ireland: No 25, Kowa Building, 8–7, Sanbancho, Chiyoda-ku (tel: (03) 3263-0695)
New Zealand: 20–40, Kamiyama-cho, Shibuya-ku (tel: (03) 3467-2271)
UK: Kinokuniya Building, 1–10–15, Kojimachi, Chiyoda-ku (tel: (03) 3265-4001)
US: 1–10–5, Akasaka, Minato-ku (tel: (03) 3583-7141)

(Abroad)

Australia: 112 Empire Circuit, Yarralomla, Canberra, ACT 2600 (tel: (02) 733-244)
Canada: 255 Sussex Drive, Ottawa, Ontario, KIN 9E6 (tel: (613) 236-8541)
New Zealand: Norwich Insurance House, 3–11 Hunter Street, Wellington 1(tel: (04) 859-020)
UK: 43–46 Grosvenor Square, London WIX 0BA (tel: (0171) 493-6030)
US: 2520 Massachusetts Avenue NW, Washington DC 20008 (tel: (202) 234-2266)

Emergency Telephone Numbers

Police: 110
Ambulance/Fire: 119
Press the red button on the telephone and dial. No money is required. The operator will answer in Japanese so you will

DIRECTORY

probably need the assistance of a Japanese speaker.
Police (general information in English): 3501-0110

Health
The Japanese have the highest life expectancy in the world. It is a clean, hygienic country and their doctors are highly trained professionals. You do not need to take any health precautions that you would not take at home. Do get health travel insurance, however, as doctors and dentists are expensive.
Clinics with English-speaking doctors include:
Hibiya Clinic, Hibiya Mitsui Building, 1–1–2 Yurakucho Chiyoda-ku, Tōkyō (tel: (03) 3502-2681)
Japan Baptist Hospital, 14 Yamanomotocho Kitashirakawa, Kyōto, Sakyo-ku (tel: (075) 781-5191)

Holidays (see **Festivals, Events and Public Holidays**, pages 109-112).

Lost Property
If you forget something or leave it in a public place there is every chance it will still be there when you return. All public transport systems including taxi companies have a lost and found service. In Tōkyō the Central Lost and Found Police Office is at 1–9–11, Koraku, Bunkyō-ku (tel: (03) 3814-4151).

Media
English-language television and radio programming is available at most large hotels. Japanese television is great fun to watch even in Japanese, and baseball and sumo, two popular television

sports, may be watched in any language. The film title and cost for viewing appear on your bill. Japan has four daily English-language newspapers, on sale in hotels or at major railway stations. There are English editions of the *Asahi*, *Yomiuri*, and *Mainichi*, the fourth is the independent *Japan Times*. The monthly English-language *Tōkyō Journal* gives comprehensive reviews and listings of theatre, film, art shows and restaurants.

Money Matters
Credit cards are widely accepted in Japan, but cash is still the preferred way of paying bills in normal transactions and the Japanese often carry huge wads of money around with them (a reflection of their safe society).
Japanese currency is the yen and there are three types of note and six different coins: 1,000, 5,000 and 10,000 yen; and 1, 5, 10, 50, 100 and 500 yen coins.
Visa, Diners Club, MasterCard and American Express are the major credit cards. Access is not very well known or accepted. Travellers cheques in yen or dollars are easily exchanged at banks or hotels. They are not readily accepted at small shops and restaurants. Rate of exchange at banks for cash and travellers cheques are invariably higher than in hotels.

Opening Times
Banks Open 09.00–15.00 hrs Mondays to Fridays; 09.00–noon Saturdays. Closed on Sundays and the second and third Saturday of each month.
Department Stores All open six

Tōkyō's bright lights

days a week at 10.00 hrs. Some stay open to 20.00 hrs although most close at 18.00 or 19.00 hrs on Saturdays, Sundays and holidays. Some are closed on Mondays, and others on Wednesdays and Thursdays.
Museums At the majority of museums you need to arrive at least half an hour before closing time to be admitted. If a national holiday falls on a museum's weekly closing day, it will be closed the following day instead.
Post Offices: see **Post Offices**
Shops Most open from around 10.00 hrs. Some close at around 18.00 hrs while others stay open much later. Many, but not all, in the central business district open on Sundays and holidays.

Personal Safety
Robbery is very rare in Japan and violent crime is even less likely. You do not need to worry about your personal safety or your belongings. Hygiene standards are high, food and tap water are safe everywhere.

Women
Japan, compared to other advanced Western nations, is a haven of freedom for women in terms of safety from male assault. Rape is almost unknown and women are able to move freely at any time of the day or night without fear of violence or theft. There is still the chance of a woman being harassed late at night by a drunken man or 'touched' in the tight confines of a rush hour subway train but a short burst of vocal abuse (in any language) would usually deal with the situation.

Pharmacies
Japanese pharmacies sell the same range of personal goods as a British chemist shop or American drug store. Pharmacies are easily found in any town. In Tōkyō there is an English-speaking chemist at the American Pharmacy, Hibiya Park

A postal logjam

Building, 1–8–1, Yurakucho, Chiyoda-ku (tel: (03) 3271-4034/5).
Open: 09.00–19.00 hrs weekdays; 11.00–18.00 hrs Saturday.
Closed: Sunday and holidays.

Places of Worship

The following churches in Tōkyō hold services in English:
Anglican: St Alban's, 3–6–25, Shibakoen, Minato-ku (tel: (03) 3431-8534)
Baptist: Tōkyō Baptist Church, 9–2, Hachiyama-cho, Shibuya-ku (tel: (03) 3461-8425)
Catholic : St Ignatius, 6–5, Kojimachi, Chiyoda-ku (tel: (03) 3263-4584)
Jewish: Jewish Community of Japan, 3–8–8, Hiro, Shibuya-ku (tel: (03) 3400-2559)

Police

Japanese policemen and women are helpful and approachable, but very few speak any English. Every Japanese district has its own police box (*koban*) usually near a busy road junction or station. The police on duty will help you find an address if you can show them a map of its location.

Post Offices

Open 09.00–17.00 hrs Monday to Friday with cash deposits/withdrawal until 15.00 hrs. Some open 09.00–12.30 hrs on Saturday. They are closed on Sunday and holidays except the main post office in each city which is open 09.00–12.30 hrs. Mail boxes are red.
Letters addressed in *romaji* sent to Japan and within Japan should have the address printed in large bold print. This makes it easier for the Japanese sorter. To post a letter or card in Japan, take it to the post office and have it weighed. Post office clerks read *romaji*. Large post offices may be used as *post restante* addresses.

Telephones

Telephones are easy to use and there are picture diagrams inside the booths showing the dialling procedure. Pay phones are different colours depending on whether they are for local calls only or for local and inter-city calls. Small red phones accept Y10 coins. They are for local calls – Y10 for one minute. Yellow and green phones accept Y10 and Y100 coins; they are for local and inter-city calls. No change is given from a Y100 coin. In big hotels and post offices there are telephones for international calls only. Green phones are also for use with pre-paid phone cards. International calls may be dialled direct or through the operator. To get the international information service dial (03) 3270-5111 (03 is not needed in Tōkyō); for the international operator, dial 0051. Dial-direct international calls as follows: 001 + the national number of the country being called + area code + local phone number. The national number of Australia is 61; Canada is 1; Ireland is 353; New Zealand is 64; UK is 44 and the US is 1. If the area code starts with a 0, omit it.

Travel Phones
The travel phone is a service provided by the Japanese government to help tourists. If you get into difficulties or need information you can use the travel phone anywhere in Japan (daily 09.00–17.00 hrs) and speak to somebody in English.
Outside Tōkyō and Kyōto, find a yellow, green or grey phone (not a red or pink one) or use a private phone. For a public phone, put in Y10 (or a phone card in green phones) and dial 0120-222-800 (or 0088-22-2800) for information on Eastern Japan; 0120-444-800 (or 0088-22-4800) for information on Western Japan. The Y10 coin or unused phone card are returned to you.
In Tōkyō and Kyōto: dial 3503-4400 for Tōkyō and 371-5649 for Kyōto. Coin(s) are not returned to you and phone cards are debited on connection.

Time
All of the islands of Japan are in the same time zone, that is nine hours ahead of Greenwich Mean Time. Daylight Saving Time is not practised.

Tipping
Tips are neither given nor expected. Large hotels and restaurants may, however, add 10 to 15 per cent (inns, or *ryokan*; 10 to 20 per cent) service charge on to your bill. There is also a

government tax on accommodation (including food and drink) of 3 per cent on accounts under 15,000 yen or 6 per cent on accounts over 15,000 yen, per person per night. Thus in hotels it is worth paying cash for meals and beverages. If the charge is added to your bill you will pay an extra 3 to 6 per cent tax.

Toilets
Many modern facilities in large towns provide Western-style toilets, but otherwise Japanese squat-type toilets are still common (see **How to be a Local**, page 104). There are public lavatories in railway stations and public parks (they do not provide paper) but those in department stores and coffee-shops are usually cleaner.

Transport
Trains
Trains are the quickest way of exploring Japan. Japan Railways (JR) run 26,000 trains daily and there are also numerous private railway lines. The fare system, however, has to be understood if you are not going to find it very expensive. There is a basic fare for whichever train you use and this is calculated by the distance you travel. Added onto this fare are various surcharges mainly dependent on how fast the train is, but also on whether you reserve a seat or not and which class you travel. There are five categories of train: the slower they are the less you pay. The *Shinkansen* are the fastest; limited stop express (*Tokkyu*) next to fastest; express (*Kyuko*) next fastest; rapid (*Kaisoku*) next to

DIRECTORY

Trains are a speedy travel option

slowest; and local trains (*Kakuekiteisha*) the slowest. For people with limited time and no strictures on their expenses, *Shinkansen* (so called 'bullet trains') are the trains to use. For the budget traveller in no rush the best trains are a combination of the limited express for long journeys and the local trains for exploring a particular area.

If you are travelling from A to B and wish to stop at places *en route*, purchase a ticket for the whole journey; you are allowed to make as many stopovers as you wish, as long as the date on your ticket remains valid for the whole journey. The period of validity is one day for 62 miles (100km), two days for 124 miles (200km) and then one day for each additional 124 miles (200km). You can get refunds on unused tickets and also change your routing once without any handling charge. If you are not sure how much your fare is or where you are going, buy the cheapest ticket from a ticket machine or ticket office and pay any balance due at the station you get off at. Most stations have a fare adjustment counter. (Reserved tickets are purchased in the railway station from the 'green-striped window' counters, called *midori-no-madoguchi* in Japanese).

Japan Rail Pass

For foreign visitors to Japan who intend to make a reasonable number of train journeys it is worth buying a Japan Rail Pass. These are valid for one, two or three weeks and can save the traveller quite a lot of money. They may only be purchased outside Japan, and they allow the user unlimited travel on all rail (except the Nozomi express), bus and ferry services. Buy a voucher from Japan Railways (JR) agents in your own country and exchange for a rail pass at Tōkyō, Osaka or other major stations on arrival, or better still at the JR counter at Narita Airport (open: 07.00–21.00 hrs daily).

Rail Travel

Other tips for travelling by train are as follows. Do not carry a lot of luggage; busy trains usually have space for only one medium-sized suitcase. Most trains have a buffet car and/or food and drink available from a trolley which is pushed up and down the aisles. They also sell *ekiben* (lunchboxes), but those sold on stalls at the station or by the sellers who run along the platform when a train stops at a station are usually cheaper and fresher. All reasonably sized stations and all those on JR lines display station names in *kanji* and *romaji* letters. The name of a station is in the middle of the nameboard with the preceding and following stations in smaller letters beneath it. Keep a careful watch for these nameboards when approaching a station. Sometimes there is only one and it can flash past before you have seen it. Avoid travelling during the rush hours (07.30–09.30 hrs and 17.00–19.00 hrs). All major stations have an information counter where you can get maps, accommodation advice and help with your train from English-speaking assistants.

Subways

The subway systems in large towns, and particularly in Tōkyō, are complicated to follow but not impossible. Before proceeding to use them visit a local tourist information office or TIC (Tourist Information Centre) in Tōkyō or Kyōto, or station information counter and get a subway map. Best of all, make your first trip with a Japanese friend. Once mastered, the subways provide a fast and cheap way of travelling about the city.

Buses

Japan has an excellent network of local city and rural buses and often the bus terminal is adjacent to the train station, so it is easy to make use of buses if you are travelling by train. For long journeys buses are slower and not significantly cheaper than trains. They are useful only for local journeys. Unfortunately buses do not show their destination in *romaji* so it is important to sort out beforehand the number of the bus you wish to take, in which direction you want to take it, and where, if at all, you need to change buses. If you do not speak Japanese, this information can be obtained from a tourist information office or a Japanese friend, but only with difficulty from a passerby on the street. Once you know your bus number and destination, write them on a piece of paper so that people can help you.

Knowing how much to pay once you are on board is much easier than catching the right bus. As you enter the bus take a ticket from the dispensing machine inside the door. It has a number on the back. A meter above the driver's head matches the cost of the fares against the numbers on

DIRECTORY

the backs of the tickets. It rotates during the bus journey, increasing the fare against the ticket numbers accordingly. (In a few instances a flat-fare is charged). As you get off, put your fare into the collecting machine by the driver's side. There is a box attached to the machine that will give change for coins and notes.

Car Hire

Car hire is widely available if you have an international driving licence, but not to be recommended. Apart from the rather complicated procedure of hiring the car, the roads are very busy, maps, if available in English, are poor, and the signposts are mainly in Japanese. That is assuming there are signposts; often there are not, and even the Japanese get lost on their own roads.

Note that traffic drives on the left.

Taxis

Taxis are metered and tipping is not a custom so you know exactly how much your journey has cost. Taxis are quite expensive but very convenient for going to a place for which you have no directions, or if you are lost. It is a good idea to carry the address and telephone number of where you are staying or going in *romaji* and *kanji*. Then you can show the address to the taxi-driver. If he gets lost he will stop the cab and ring for directions.

Tourist Offices
Japanese National Tourist Organisation (JNTO)
Australia: Level 33, The Chifley Tower, 2 Chifley Square, Sydney, NSW 2000 (tel: (02) 232-4522)
Canada: 165 University Avenue, Toronto, Ontario M5H 3B8 (tel: (416) 366-7140)
UK: 167 Regent Street, London W1R 7FD (tel: (0171) 734-9638/9)
US: Rockfeller Plaza, 630 Fifth Avenue, Suite 2101, New York 10111 (tel: (212) 757-5640). Also offices in Chicago, Dallas, Los Angeles and San Francisco
Japan: 10-1 Yurakucho 2-chome, Chiyoda-ku, Tōkyō 100 (tel: (03) 3216-1901)

Tourist Information Centres (TIC)

Open: 09.00–17.00 hrs weekdays, 09.00–12.00hrs Saturdays (Tōkyō Airport, daily 09.00–20.00 hrs). They have English-speaking staff who are most helpful when you arrive in Japan. They will give advice on travel arrangements and accommodation. The centres stock lots of useful free literature. There are four:

In Tōkyō
Kontani Building, 6–6 Yurakucho 1-chome, Chiyoda-ku (tel: (03) 3502-1461)
Tōkyō International Airport: Terminal 1, Narita, Chiba 282 (tel: (0476) 32-8711)
Terminal 2, Narita, Chiba 282 (tel: (0476) 34-6251)

In Kyōto
Kyōto Tower Building, Higashi-Shiokojicho, Shimogy-ku (tel: (075) 371-5649)

Travel Agencies

There are many travel agencies in every city in Japan. JNTO or TIC offices listed above will provide you with a list of JATA (Japanese Association of Travel Agents) approved agents.

LANGUAGE

To learn to write their own language the Japanese must master four ways of writing: kanji, hiragana, katakana and romaji. *Kanji* are Chinese characters, *hiragana* are Japanese characters used to link kanji ideograms, *katakana* is used to write foreign words and *romaji* uses the Roman alphabet to write Japanese. Nowadays most Japanese can read and write romaji, and in large cities many important landmarks and street signs will be given in romaji as well as kanji. The Japanese spend many years at school learning English but very few are confident of speaking it. They are often much better at understanding the spoken word than at reading and writing it. The following Japanese phrases are amongst those most helpful to a visitor.

Basic Phrases
Mr/Ms
...san after the surname (but don't ever append it to your own name)
Yes
hai
Yes, I am listening
hai, hai
Yes, I agree
hai, so des
Thank you
(domo) arigato
Yes please
hai onegaishimasu
No (rarely used)
iie
No, I disagree
chigaimas
I'm sorry
gomen-nasai

Excuse me (also used to call waiter)
sumimasen...
Good morning
o-haiyo-gozaimasu
Good afternoon
konnichi-wa
Good evening
konban-wa
Good night
oya-sumi-nasai
Goodbye
sayonara
Excuse me, do you speak English?
sumimasen, Eigo hanashimasu-ka?
Please (help yourself) (etc)
dozo
Please give me...
...okudasai
Yes, just a little
hai, sukoshi dake
No, I can't
ie, dame desu
On starting a meal
itadakimas
Cheers!
kampai!
Thank you (for kindness)
domo arigato gozaimash'ta
Thank you (after a meal)
gochiso-sama desh'ta
What is your name?
o-namae-wa?
My name is 'Smith'
watashi wa 'Smith' desu
Are you Mr/Ms 'Smith'?
'Smith'-san desu ka?

Accommodation
How much is it?
...ikura desu ka?
nightly
ippaku
weekly
isshuukan
for bed and breakfast
choshokutsuki

LANGUAGE

for full board
sanshokutsuki
excluding meals
sudomari desu
does that include...?
...wat suite imasu-ka?
meals
shokuji
service
saabisu
Have you anything cheaper?
Nani ka motto yasui no wa
(arimasen ka?)

Food and Drink
How much is it?
ikura desu ka?
Breakfast, please
'morning service' (*or*) Choshoku
o kudasai
Lunch, please
Chuushoku o kudasai
Dinner, please
Yuushoku o kudasai
It tastes good
oishi desu
It doesn't taste good
oi shi-ku nai desu
Menu, please
menu o kudasai
Bill, please
kanjo onegaishimasu
Do you accept credit cards?
credit cardo tsukaemasu ka?
coffee-shop
kissaten
restaurant
restoran
beer
biru
Japanese sake
o-sake (*or* Nihon-shu)
water
mizu
milk
milku
coffee
kohee
Indian tea
kocha
Japanese or Chinese tea
ocha
sugar, please
sato, kudasai

Emergencies
(I'm) ill
(watashi wa) byooki desu
Get a doctor
Oisha-san o yonde kudasai
quickly
hayaku
danger
kiken
It's dangerous!
Abunai!
Fire!
Kaji!
Help!
tasukete (kudasai)!
Hospital
Byooin
Police
Keisatsu

Train Travel
At what time does the train for Tōkyō leave?
Tōkyō yuki no densha wa nanji
ni demasu ka?
From which platform?
Nanban sen kara demasu ka?
Where is platform 1?
Ichi ban sen wa doko desuka?
Does the train for Osaka leave from here?
Osaka yuki no densha wa koko
kara demasu ka?
I want to get off at Tōkyō Station.
Tōkyō eki de oritai desu.
Will you tell me when to get off?
Itsu oritara yoi ka oshiete
kudasai? (*or*)
Eki de oroshite kudasai.
How many stations (before) I get off?
Koko kara nanbanme no eki
desu-ka?

INDEX

INDEX

The Automobile Association would like to thank the following photographers,
libraries and associations for their assistance in the preparation of this book.

DOUGLAS CORRANCE took all the photographs in this book (© AA Photo Library)
except:

JAPANESE NATIONAL TOURIST ORGANISATION 41 Ito Spa, 64 Kumamoto Castle,
76 Towadu-ko, 111 Ose Myojin Festival, 114 Sumo wrestling.

MARY EVANS PICTURE LIBRARY 11 Shogun Minamoto Jorimoto.

NATURE PHOTOGRAPHERS LTD 87 Crane (S C Bisserot).

SPECTRUM COLOUR LIBRARY Cover Japanese Child, 36 Mt Fuji, 66/7 Okinawa
Coast, 79 Hokkaidō, 84 Ashino-ko.

Author's Acknowledgements

The author would like to thank all the staff of the London office of the Japan National
Tourist Organisation for the assistance they have given him over a number of years
in planning various trips to Japan. Sometimes the requests have been out of the
ordinary (eccentric one could say), but the staff have never been less than polite
and prepared to help.

Copy editor for original edition: Helen Douglas-Cooper.
For this revision: Copy editor and verifier Colin Follett.
Thanks also to David Scott for his updating work on this revised edition.